THE M

OF WINNING TEAMS

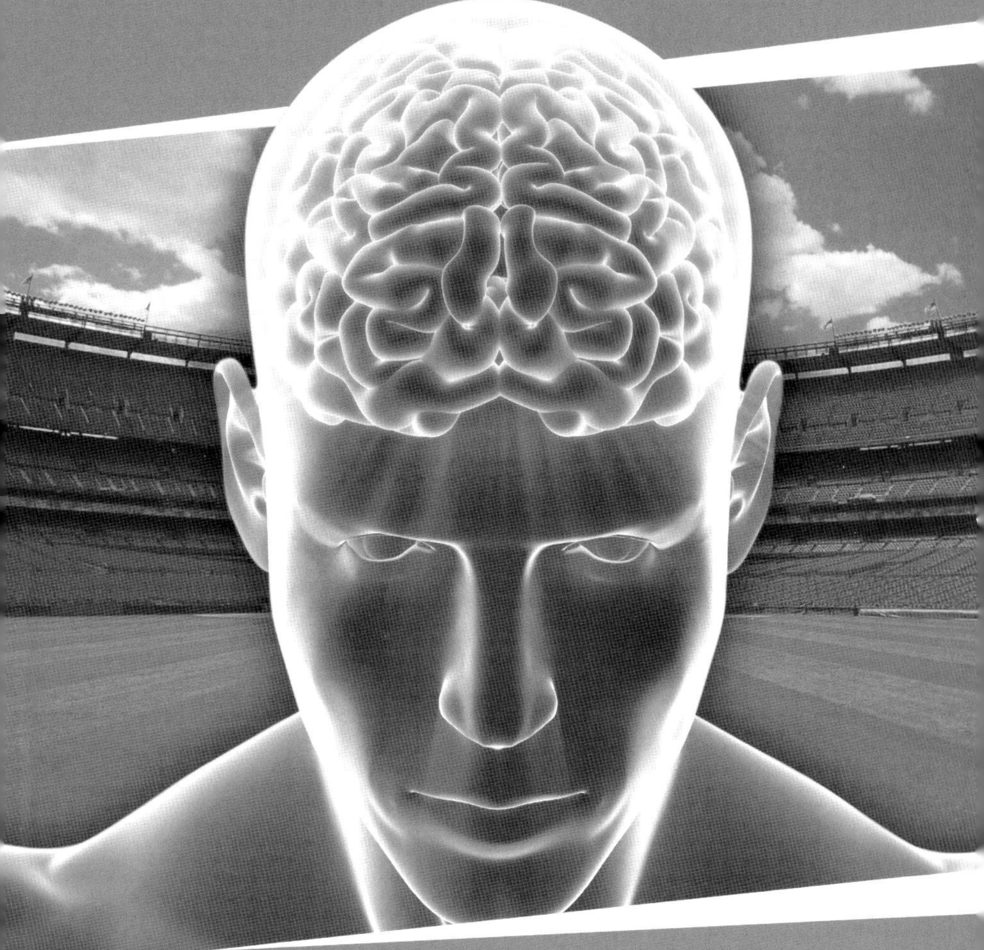

CREATING TEAM SUCCESS THROUGH
ENGAGEMENT & CULTURE

RICHARD MALONEY

First published by Busybird Publishing 2014

Founding Director – Premiership Coach (Sport), Engage & Grow (Business) and Quality Mind (Industry Leaders and Elite Athletes).

ISBN 978-0-9924874-9-2

Cover design by Ben Durant

Layout and typesetting: Jason Farrugia

Busybird Publishing
PO Box 855
Eltham Victoria
Australia 3095

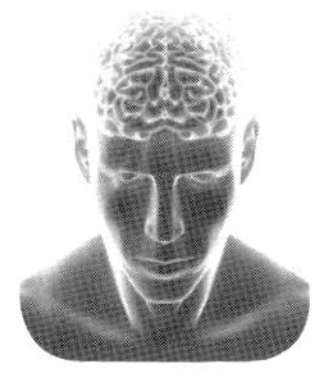

TABLE OF CONTENTS

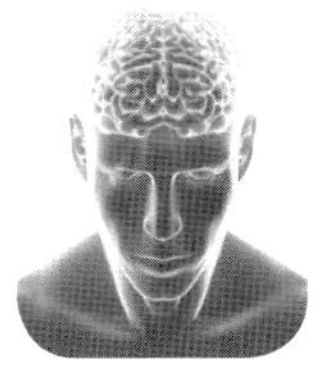

DEDICATION

This book is dedicated to my parents, Peter and Heather Maloney. Thank you for hauling me around all over town as a junior to play sport, and for the amazing level of love and support you have always shown me.

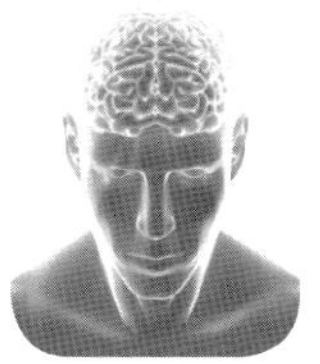

FOREWORD

All of the information in this book, aside from the personal opinions and experiences of the guest experts, derive from my own personal experiences and from a specialist group of great minds that are involved in promoting a greater level of intelligence, to which I am a representative of.

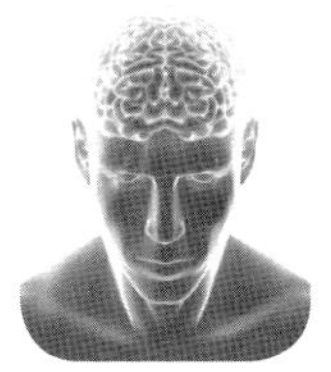

ABOUT THE AUTHOR

Having been involved in 39 Grand Finals for 24 'Premierships' or 'Championships' in the sports industry, Richard Maloney understands how important it is to have all levels of an organisation 'flowing', be it in sport or in business.

Richard specialises in the development of high performance teams, individuals and organisations in both business and sport. He has 10 years experience as an established leader in sports management, commercial management and executive leadership coaching. This includes both corporate and SME markets, with organisations such as Fremantle Football Club, Western Bulldogs Football Club (AFL) and TEAMelbourne (Melbourne FC AFL, Melbourne Storm NRL, Melbourne Racing Club, Melbourne Tigers NBL, Melbourne Vixens Netball).

Richard's focus is on leadership, executive development, organisational engagement and culture. He comes accredited as an educator and trainer, high performance coach and NLP master practitioner with a passion for the creation and development of business leaders, executives, elite athletes and teams.

He also has a proven sporting and business background as a successful leader with a list of accomplishments in a range of management positions. Richard has worked in twelve different industries and is the Director of Premiership Coach (elite sport), Engage and Grow (business) and Quality Mind (industry leaders and elite athletes).

With Engage & Grow, Richard leads a united team of seven national and international Certified Business Coaches. They specialise in advancing 'somewhat engaged' team members into 'fully engaged' leaders.

Here are some of Richard Maloney's accomplishments:

Fitzroy FC, VAFA, Leadership and Culture Coach, Pending, 2014

Deniliquin Rover FC PDFL, Leadership and Culture Coach, Pending, 2014

Red Hill FC MPNFL, Leadership and Culture Coach, Pending, 2014

Melbourne Cricket Club VPC, Leadership and Culture Consultant, Finalists, 2013-14

Western Bulldogs FC AFL, Leadership and Culture Coach, 2011-12-13

Yarra Valley Old Boys FC VAFA, Leadership and Culture Coach, Grand Finalists, 2013

Elsternwick FC VAFA, Leadership and Culture Coach, Grand Finalists, 2013

Montmorency FC NFL, Leadership and Culture Coach, Grand Finalists, 2013

Upwey Tecoma FC YVFL, Leadership and Culture Coach, 2 Grand Finalists, 2013

Caulfield Bears FC SFL, Leadership and Culture Coach, 2013

Caulfield Grammarians FC VAFA, Leadership and Culture Coach, 2013

Loan Market South Melbourne, Executive Leadership and Culture Coach, 2013

Edge Financial Planning, Executive Leadership and Culture Coach, 2013

Melbourne Cricket Club VPC, Leadership and Culture Coach, 7 x Premiership, 2012-13

Upwey Tecoma Cricket Club YVCL, Leadership and Culture Coach, 2 x Premierships, 2012-13

Parkdale Vultures FC VAFA, Leadership and Culture Coach, 3 x Premierships, 2011-12

Upwey Tecoma FC YVFL, Leadership and Culture Coach, Grand Finalists, 2013

Moora Warriors FC WACFL WA, Leadership and Culture Coach, Premiership winners, 2012

Papunya FC CAFL NT, Leadership and Culture Coach, Finalists, 2012

Greensborough FC NFL, Leadership and Culture Coach, 2012

Old Mentonians FC VAFA, Leadership and Culture Coach, 2012

Santa Teresa FC CAFL NT, Leadership and Culture Coach, Grand Finalists, 2012

Prahran-Assumption FC VAFA, Leadership and Culture Consultant, Grand Finalists, 2012

Cranbourne FC MPNFL, Leadership and Culture Coach, 2 x Grand Finalists, 2011

Upwey Tecoma FC YVFL, Leadership and Culture Coach, Finalists, 2012

Hermannsburg FC CAFL NT, Leadership and Culture Coach, Premiership winners, 2012

Subiaco FC WAFL WA, Leadership and Culture Coach, 2012

Ivanhoe FC VAFA, Leadership and Culture Coach, 2 x Grand Finalists, 2012

Mentone Grammar School, Leadership and Culture Consultant, 2012

Williamstown FC VFL, Leadership and Culture Coach, Grand Finalists, 2010-11

South Croydon FC EFL, Leadership and Culture Coach, 2011

South Fremantle Colts FC, Leadership and Culture Coach, 2 x Premierships, 2011-12

West Broken Hill FC BHFC NSW, Leadership and Culture Coach, Finalists, 2011-12

Cranbourne FC MPFL, Leadership and Culture Coach, Premiership winners, 2011

Prahran-Assumption FC VAFA, Leadership and Culture Coach, Premiership winners, 2011

CBC St. Kilda, Leadership and Culture Consultant, 2011-12-13

De La Salle College, Leadership and Culture Consultant, 2011-12-13

Emmanuel College, Leadership and Culture Consultant, 2011-12-13

Mazenod College, Leadership and Culture Consultant, 2011-12-13

Parade College, Leadership and Culture Consultant, 2011-12-13

Salesian College, Leadership and Culture Consultant, 2011-12-13

Simonds Catholic College, Leadership and Culture Consultant, 2011-12-13

St. Bedes College, Leadership and Culture Consultant, 2011-12-13

St. Josephs College, Leadership and Culture Consultant, 2011-12-13

Whitefriars College, Leadership and Culture Consultant, 2011-12-13

Bright FC OKFL, Leadership and Culture Coach, Finalists, 2011-12-13

Melbourne University Blues FC VAFA, Assistant Coach, Finalists, 2008-2009

Coffs Harbor City Council NSW, Executive Leadership and Culture Coach, 2009-2010

Mildura Rural City Council NSW, Executive Leadership and Culture Coach, 2009-2010

Greater Shepparton City Council VIC, Executive Leadership and Culture Coach, 2009-2010

Port Stephens Council NSW, Executive Leadership and Culture Coach, 2009-2010

Ararat Rural City Local Government VIC, Executive Leadership and Culture Coach, 2009-2010

Melbourne Tigers NBL, TEAMelbourne Commercial Manager, 2007-08

Melbourne Vixens NA, TEAMelbourne Commercial Manager, 2007-08

Melbourne Demons AFL, TEAMelbourne Commercial Manager, 2007-08

Melbourne Storm NRL, TEAMelbourne Commercial Manager, 2007-08

Melbourne Racing Club, TEAMelbourne Commercial Manager, 2007-08

Perth FC WAFL, Board Member - Director of Football, 2005-06-07

Fremantle Football Club AFL, Commercial Partnerships Senior Executive, 2005-06-07

WA Country State Team Representative WACFL, 2005

Subiaco FC WAFL, Premiership Captain, 2004

Subiaco FC WAFL, Club Captain, Grand Finalists, 2003

WA State Team, WAFL, Vice Captain, 2003

WA State Team, Representative, WAFL, 2001-02

Subiaco FC, Best and Fairest, WAFL, 2001

Subiaco Junior FC, Coach U/14, Finalists, 2001

Norm Goss Medallist (Premiership best player award) VFL, 2000

Sandringham FC VFL, Premiership winners, 2000

Southport FC QAFL, 2 x Premierships, 1997-98

St Kilda FC, AFL Rookie Listed Player, 1995

Beaumaris FC VAFA, Premiership winners, 1995

Sandringham FC VFA, Premiership winners, 1994

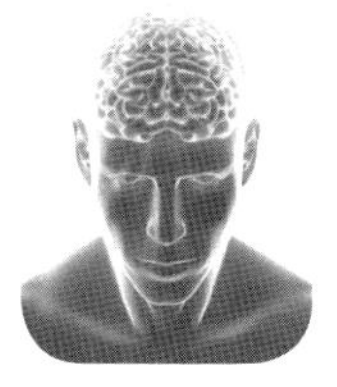

TESTIMONIALS

'I would definitely recommend Richard Maloney's program. It has been of massive benefit to me individually, and to the team. We have gone to another level with our leadership in a very short amount of time. I have also seen a significant positive change to our club's culture.'

– Matthew Boyd, Past Captain, Western Bulldogs FC, AFL

'Richard Maloney was our keynote speaker at our annual MLC Business Intervention Workshop in May 2014. The official feedback from the 32 business owners was outstanding. 83% of the group rated Richard a 9/10, with the balance rating him a 10/10. Richard demonstrated high levels of energy, conviction, and he was a true professional with his preparation and ultimate delivery on the day. I highly recommend any and all business owners to engage with Richard as he has a unique message and an ability to authentically assimilate, engage and inspire!'

– John Campagna, National Australia Bank

'I can categorically say that I learned more about leadership in three months with Richard's program than I did in seven years in a leadership role as a player in the AFL.'

– Daniel Cross, Melbourne FC, AFL

'Engage & Grow has been a resounding success at Edge FP. It has created an environment of care, growth and built a foundation for perpetual success. The program has allowed us to identify exactly who are the people in our team, and given every individual the opportunity to shine and grow as themselves. Importantly however, as everyone within the team embraced the program, we began to get some traction and identify exactly what it is we stand for as a business. No matter the stage of your business's cycle, Engage & Grow will drive a committed, engaged and happy workforce. Within 12 weeks we also effortlessly improved our profitability by 21% with Richard's program.'

– Leigh Stafford, CEO, Edge Financial Planning

'Richard Maloney's program was massive for us as it turned our season around. I don't think we would have won back-to-back premierships without it to be honest! It got guys committed and it changed the club. We basically went from having one captain to seven or eight in a short amount of time. We will definitely be rolling it out again every year from here on in. 10/10.'

– Sam Radford, Head Coach, Parkdale FC

'I had the good fortune to work with Richard on a sensitive project that required deep insight and a thorough understanding of his subject in 2013. After a period of 12 months the end result has more than met my expectations. Richard delivered as he said he

would. I would have no hesitation to recommend Richard to provide a change management program that requires commitment and delivers. Thanks Richard.'

– Gary Posner, Director, The Global Beauty Group

'We had factions within the ranks in previous years and now we are united as one. Our social events have improved out of sight and the players have really enjoyed being involved. It has definitely changed our club for the better and it played a big role in our premiership success this year.'

– Bill King, Assistant Coach, Cranbourne FC

'Richard, thank you so very much for introducing and rolling out such a successful leadership and engagement program in 2012, the likes of which had never been seen before at our football club. I must admit it took some work to convince the committee to come on board and invest in the program initially but I know they now strongly believe that player leadership, engagement and true ownership of the football club are at an all time high and will only continue to grow in the future. I couldn't feel happier and prouder or more vilified in my decision to pursue this program!'

– Glen Spence, Head Coach, Upwey Tecoma Football and Netball Club

'At the start of working with Richard Maloney we had no leaders other than those appointed to official positions. 18 weeks later we now have eight more quality trained leaders, and a thriving culture!'

– Andrew Kent, Melbourne Cricket Club

'I found Richard Maloney's program to be stimulating and challenging. I liked the way it brought out the best in some of the quieter and more reserved staff members. The bond between staff and departments has grown and personally I'm much more aware of how my actions affect others … both good and bad. It's been a thoroughly worthwhile experience. We also improved our bottom line profitability by an impressive 47% by the end of the 12 hour program.'

– Toby Edmunds, CEO, Loan Market Franchisee, South Melbourne

'Due to Richard Maloney's program I witnessed considerable change and improvements in our club's culture. There was more ownership of the club by the players, greater level of respect for teammates on field and a higher level of professionalism. I rate the program 9/10.'

– Stephen McCrystal, Leadership Facilitator, Ivanhoe AFC

'For the first time in my football career I've noticed a tighter bond between players on field. There is a real sense of teamwork and ambition amongst all the players as compared to the beginning of the year. I also have a newfound confidence in being assertive as a leader.'

– Sam Johnson, Old Mentone Grammarians FC

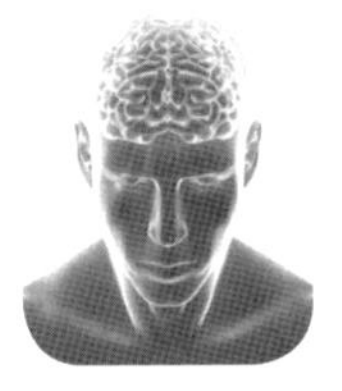

INTRODUCTION

After many years of participation in sport at all levels, and working within twelve different industries, it is abundantly clear that most teams work *hard* but not *smart*.

There is a discernable need for new ideas and practices!

The industry standard for mainstream leadership training has had its day. 70% of the Australian workforce is disengaged; and mainstream leadership courses usually prove to be a waste of time and money. It is undeniably evident that these high levels of disengagement in Australia and throughout the world demonstrate the need for change.

The ideas put forward in this book are focused on the maximisation of team *engagement*. Once achieved, new leaders will emerge, and they will often be the people you least expect!

Engagement uncovers leaders, and creates a thriving culture. This will in turn provide personal, emotional and financial rewards.

Encouraging high performance athletes and business leaders to *go within* and unlock true potential by eliminating self-belief is a necessary step if they want to be the very best in their chosen sport or profession.

Self-belief can only get an elite performer so far. The next stage is *knowing* what you're capable of, not just *believing*. This creates a cascading effect of higher energy levels never before experienced, leading to a greater balance of the three key life elements: health, wealth and relationships.

The principles outlined in this book apply equally to the stadium and the boardroom.

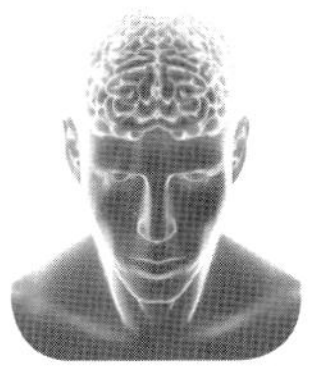

CHAPTER 1

How To Create Massive Change

It's a given that people rarely follow advice, even when it's good for them! We see examples everywhere – we are told by doctors to stop smoking, limit drinking, lose weight or make lifestyle changes. However even when faced with an immediate threat, we rarely change our behaviours.

This is because we are creatures of habit who crave constant familiarity in life. These habits are coded to keep us safe, meaning we rarely get uncomfortable enough to grow. This is the reason there are so few leaders in life, because to be a great leader you must continually get yourself into uncomfortable situations where you are forced to grow mentally. We also possess strands of DNA passed on from our ancestors that do and do not serve us. This DNA has its tentacles firmly routed into our system, and forms part of what we are today.

For example, I was recently forced to terminate one of my clients, as they were simply not prepared to do the work necessary to improve their situation. They had a degree of pain; they knew the course that needed to be taken; they clearly understood the why and the how;

but they simply couldn't take that necessary leap. They wanted me the coach to do the hard yards, not themselves. After six meetings I had to remove myself. My client wanted to be number one in their industry, and they were on the way up. However as the pressure mounted, the climb became far too great and it was a one step forward three steps back situation. I can't do the hard yards for others. How can you solve someone's problems when they are the problem and they don't want to change?

The client must design his or her own path. As a coach, I simply shine a brighter light on the path to which they must walk.

The three key fundamentals to making leaders are:

I) Adversity in life

II) Continual laser leadership training

III) Experience on the job.

The key fundamentals I focus on in this book are II and III.

When I ask my clients what they think leadership is, the same answers always come back. Most will provide accurate examples of attributes a leader should and shouldn't possess. They know what it takes to be a leader, and they readily want to change their behaviours to advance themselves. They just haven't.

In my experience there are four key reasons why the majority of leadership programs are ineffective:

1. The training focuses on the individual, not the organisation and the individual.

2. They are only made available for c-suite or middle management.
3. New individual and group leadership habits are not measured and made accountable on a daily basis.
4. Most leadership training is just theory based 'knowledge dumping', and not lived through, especially in a world where our minds are already overwhelmed.

Leadership theory based 'knowledge dumping' such as personality profiling, 360-degree assessments, 1, 2, or 3-day or monthly workshops and meditation are just a few common methods used to promote leadership and improve engagement in the workplace. They all have their place in the training game, but to gain maximum traction, there is a new, faster and more effective method. It's called 'leadership living' and all levels of the organisation participate together in the workplace. It is an all action methodology, which means team members will live, breathe and grow together as a united force. It breeds true engagement, uncovers more leaders and flows on via a waterfall effect to build a powerful and united culture.

Mainstream leadership and management training courses can be great in their delivery, and they do serve a purpose. Usually the chosen leaders who are seen to have potential are given the opportunity to attend an external course. While these courses can be extremely inspiring when you're there, it's like taking a dirty fish from a dirty pond, cleaning it down with new teachings and returning it to the dirty pond. The goal of course, is for the newly cleaned fish to come back and clean the dirty pond. However a few days after a clean fish returns to a dirty pond it inevitably loses momentum and becomes dirty once again – the pond is far too big and too dirty for one fish to clean on its own, or with the small group that also participated in the cleansing.

'Great leadership is all about taking action, authentically and charismatically.'

Assisting Change

The question was put to me recently 'Can change be achieved easily and effortlessly?' As human beings we change from the moment of conception. We have learnt to talk, learnt to walk, achieved various goals, secured employment, met new people – the list goes on and on. All of these new experiences involved change at one level or another. To think that change is difficult or easy is all in the eye of the individual. Something that may be difficult for one person may be easy for another. Change becomes more challenging for people when they are in conflict. People will remain in their jobs and relationships when they are unhappy because of the fear of the unknown.

So when people have trouble initiating change, there is usually some kind of conflict at play at a deeper level. This is where Neuro-Linguistic Programming (NLP) is a very powerful tool that can assist people in making fast and effective change. Understanding the seven key neurological motivators can also play a significant role in speeding up the process.

NLP is an exceptionally influential discipline that enables people to unblock the structures of human communication and human excellence. By doing so people can think, communicate and manage themselves, and others, more effectively. NLP is a highly effective change-management tool that transforms the way people think, and it is without doubt one of the most powerful skills used in business management, mind training, sales, sports coaching and all forms of personal development.

NLP explores the relationships between how we think (neuro), how we communicate (linguistic) and our patterns of behaviour and emotion (programs).

By studying and learning from these relationships, people can effectively transform the way they traditionally think and act, adopting new and far more successful models of human excellence.

It is proven that NLP has a role to play, and it is an effective change creation tool, however, there is an even more advanced methodology, and we will further touch on it later in this book.

It is very important to also understand that there are seven neurological motivators that when tapped in to, also help to create the change we are after. These are crucial for those who want success, and want it fast:

1. Pain
2. Pleasure
3. Reward
4. Recognition
5. Self improvement
6. Self direction
7. Transcendent purpose

What we feel is influenced by what we truly value. It is one or more of these seven motivators that creates the ability to effectively motivate people to achieve peak performance in work, sport and life.

Through NLP we learn that every behaviour has a positive intention. By 'positive' I mean purposeful – it's trying to achieve something. This is a really compelling way of looking at the world, especially as a performance coach.

Your values are your unconscious motivators, and all highly successful men and women have one thing in common – they are strongly and consciously aware of their values.

Mixing these in with leadership training is a must to ensure individual and collective change. This is when your return on investment will be well and truly realised.

These seven neurological touch points stem from three different parts of the brain:

- **Neocortex** – Thought (including planning, language, logic and will, awareness)
- **Limbic System** – Emotion (feelings, relationship/nurturing, images and dreams, play)
- **Reptilian Brain** – Instinct (survival, breathing/swallowing/heartbeat, startle response)

These three parts of the brain intermingle and communicate, sometimes like a contentious committee. The Neocortex likes to think it's in the driver's seat, but the Limbic System and Reptilian Brain exercise a lot of power. The Reptilian Brain, by far the oldest and simplest, is responsible for our survival, but its choices are limited.

Who vs What Leadership Development[1]

One of the best ways to combat the issues that continually arise from traditional leadership training (for example; loss of momentum afterwards) is to implement a different type of development. It's what I call '*who* development'.

While '*what* development' is focused on adding new knowledge and skills to the leader and making him or her more knowledgeable, *who* development is about working with the leaders to empty their knowledge cup.

This is done by digging in to the history of the leader and pinpointing why they have become the way they are, based on childhood mental patterning. When the leader's cup gets emptied and an understanding takes place of *who* they are, instead of *what* they are or have become, then new springs of energy and inspiration kick in. This process is much more effective than adding more knowledge to the 'cup of life'.

In this *who* model individual skills and situations are irrelevant – it is solely about instilling in the leader a new mental software package that will allow them to develop into their best selves. While it can be a rather challenging journey, the program I have developed has identified several key components responsible for acquiring this quality mind. In this book I offer several strategies high performers and leaders can use straight away.

We do not offer a quick fix panacea or band-aid solutions either. When offering the fundamentals, we need to be patient and willing to do the digging. This needs to be done with trained guidance, and it's a sure way of creating a successful winning team and becoming an authentic and influential leader.

1. Centre For Creative Leadership (CCL) runs with a similar model called Vertical vs Horizontal Leadership Development, see www.ccl.org

Through the process, you might discover that the leader needs to become more assertive, or that they need to listen to team members more, or that they require greater confidence when identifying and resolving problems.

The emerging leader will often come back with a reason or a motivation behind their unresourceful behaviours. It could be that they feel unhappy with their careers or the direction their life has taken. It could be that their role has changed too much for them to cope and maintain passion for their work, or that being a leader isn't what they thought it would be. The emerging leader might have been a successful autonomous individual, but is not experiencing the same success when it comes to leadership.

In many cases during our programs, it is found that the leadership style of the person in charge is a bit too heavy-handed for everyone else, and that the other members of the team are too fearful to speak up or do anything to change the situation. This is an example of why engagement levels can swiftly plummet.

This very common heavy-handed approach rarely works, because we are dealing with adults who already have entrenched ways of thinking about themselves and the world! Telling them that they are lacking in areas and need to make up for gaps in their knowledge can easily be handled poorly. It can sometimes create conflict where none was necessary in the first place, and doesn't usually help at all in the long term.

A common concern is that leaders are not empowering. That they don't listen to their team members or seek their opinions and ideas. Sometimes leaders need to not only empower their team members with words, but to empower them by delegating more tasks and responsibilities to them. A true leader should step back and allow their team to step up from time to time. We all need to feel valued.

Who leadership development is a fast and highly effective strategy which assists individuals in clearing their past. This method assists these leaders in rebuilding a firm foundation of mental clarity by emptying their mental wastebasket first. They will then quickly understand that their old habits were only holding them back. This is where we witness inspirational and long-term growth. This is *Who* leadership development, and it is the new way to attain change far quicker than traditional knowledge dumping methods. By participating in one of our programs, we are able to expose leaders' weaknesses and unproductive beliefs to rebuild them from the ground up.

Self-Challenge

In many cases people who go through an intensive, transforming leadership experience – one that leads to winning team success – come back and say that the greatest challenge for them was changing their identity. They had to admit that they had been trapped and unable to develop or advance further because they were so entrenched in older ways of thinking: assumptions, beliefs, and their overall identity from the past. Once they were able to let go of all of these factors and create an identity that they liked for themselves, they were able to progress and grow rapidly, becoming a more valuable contributor to the winning team.

The method I employ in my leadership program requires those taking part to identify the behaviours that worked for them in the past, but are not serving them so well right now. 'How is that working for you?' This is a simple question that can take people a long way when they really start reflecting internally! If one can honestly self-critique by looking within and asking themselves this question, they can strip back old beliefs and behaviors where necessary, and make the changes needed to become capable of winning team success.

To truly send the message home and avoid any loss of momentum, participants in our programs continue to be monitored and supported once they have completed our programs and are back in the workplace. The coach and other people working on their development need to follow up and check in on a regular basis, as well as help the leader set up an internal network that can help keep them on the right road to success.

This approach works particularly well in team cultures where change will be difficult. When an emerging leader does not possess real power, it's imperative to ensure that they have a close, personal network within their team that will help them out when they come up against resistance within the organisation.

Individual Ownership

Leaders who participate in the program also experience the realisation that it is no longer the organisation's responsibility to manage their development, but their own. Surprisingly this is still a big issue in elite sport and big business. Many organisations send their players and team members on external courses and leadership programs that they don't even want to attend! Emerging leaders can feel as if they are some kind of reluctant bystander in their own professional development, and therefore take part in development opportunities provided purely to 'tick a box'. This is what we are changing, and it's working. A true leader will regularly look within, and will take sole and whole responsibility for their own personal and professional development.

Public Accountability and Developmental Network

Being publicly accountable and surrounding yourself with a strong support network are important factors in ensuring ongoing and long-lasting change in an emerging leader. First, they need to make public their goals and what they intend to achieve. This is crucial, and opens up many opportunities. Next, they need to create a developmental network for themselves that crosses into and out of the team. This could be support within the team in the form of a senior manager, or external support in the form of a coach who works with them on a couple of issues at a time, in a specialised way. It's essential to follow through with these if you want to safeguard long-term leadership success.

Although public accountability seems a terrifying prospect for many people, in doing so they will realise great benefits. If you make your goals public in a team or organisational setting, then you are opening yourself up to opportunities and maximum growth. Others in the team may want to help you achieve your goals, or they can give you feedback on how things can be done in a better way. You are creating and maintaining dialogue about the individual and the organisation; and the accountability can be quite contagious!

I was recently coaching a GM of Marketing who was struggling to maintain the level of energy and enthusiasm required to effectively lead his team. Managing and overseeing strategy and staff morale were two of his key responsibilities, and as part of the program he was provided with honest feedback from his team members. They felt that while he was highly knowledgeable and a great inclusion culturally to the organisation, he needed to step up his efforts when it came to leading his team, providing direction, being more present and delivering on agreed workflow deadlines. Once he received this feedback, we created a Road Map action plan together to ensure his motivation and focus shifted to meet his team's feedback. As part of the plan, he had to approach two highly regarded General Managers (one from within his organisation and one from outside) and ask them to act as his advisors. Both GMs agreed to meet with him fortnightly for lunch (he was buying) and the GM of Marketing then reported back to the group and made his Road Map action plan public. Before we knew it, his communication and productivity had improved dramatically, and they now had a more hands on, engaged and approachable leader! This had a ripple effect that generated enthusiasm, communication, inspiration and collaboration within the team.

Leadership is Not Heroic

Why is that? The simple answer is that individual heroics are an egotistical illusion. While it's good to recognise the achievements of individuals, in most cases their achievements are part of a team effort with an extensive background support network. Many people think that leadership is about emulating the life of famous achievers from the past and present, but they will often fail to recognise the individual efforts of everyone who worked as a collective to obtain that result.

In the real world, it's just too complicated and difficult for an emerging leader or coach to be the person who is there all the time, who solves all of the problems and takes responsibility for everything by themselves. Few can do this kind of work well on their own. On the contrary, the most effective approach is for everyone to share the responsibilities and for everyone to share the same vision. The goal of leadership should be to become viral – a true leader wants to create more leaders and will fill the team with emerging leaders to ensure this.

This is a key to winning team success!

It's far too easy for one person to give up when the going gets too tough, so it's better to share the burden across as many team members as possible, while maintaining the same goals. This can be done by allowing people to use global strategies, such as depending on each other, that can cross all cultural and generational boundaries.

Empowering leaders with the tools to help them find direction, to stand behind that direction and drive others towards it is vital. This (along with an unwavering commitment from all participants in the program) is the key goal of the work that I do with our clients across the country.

Unexpected Relief

Another positive consequence of this type of training is the great sense of relief that usually results once responsibilities start to be delegated, and previously insurmountable tasks just get done. When people begin to understand that the work that they do is not special, and can easily be shared by others, it can be very liberating. 'A problem shared is a problem halved'.

Leaders feel an immense weight lifted from their shoulders when the stress and pressure they've formerly experienced solo is shared amongst the group. It also brings with it a stronger sense of 'team' and a closeness and camaraderie that may have been missing. Everyone in a team has something to offer and contribute, and they should be rounded up and delegated tasks to achieve this relieving effect. When there is no single authority figure, then everybody starts developing his or her own sense of responsibility and commitment. We also witness a sense of achievement and pride amongst the team when these new systems are proving to work, which brings with it fresh levels of energy.

How to Quickly Improve Your Team's Leadership Skills

Gather your leaders and discuss how your team believes others perceive them outside of the team (this may be the general public, your competitors, and others within the organisation).

On sticky notes, have each team member individually note their concerns, and how they think the team and the organisation can be improved going forward.

Go through each note publicly (sticking them on a white board or a wall) and circle the top two or three issues. These should be addressed first.

Some examples of the issues that are commonly raised are:

- Lack of communication.
- Inconsistency when it comes to behaviours.
- The environment is negative or not enjoyable.
- We don't share enough information with each other.
- It's an us against them mentality.

Once the top issues are agreed upon as a team, the group should then agree on an area of focus to improve upon each week. Ask each leader what they want to do, personally, to fix these issues. At the end of the meeting each leader will be held accountable for:

1. 1 x Weekly *Group* Leadership Act
2. 1 x Weekly *Individual* Leadership Act

The agreed focus point must be tangible and actionable. For example, if the area of focus for the week is 'lack of communication', a weekly group leadership act could be each leader taking the time to learn one interesting thing about someone in the group that they didn't already know. The leaders must then report back to the group and share these new and interesting facts with the broader group at the weekly meeting. The team should repeat this each week until everyone has a greater understanding of who their fellow team members are.

An individual leadership act could be improving on time management, completing certain work flow deadlines or taking ownership of a social work event. At each meeting the leaders will all be required to again report back to the group on how they went with their key deliverables.

The main reason we get the leaders to focus on these tangible leadership acts is to create new and sustainable resources and habits – both individually and collectively. Once new habits are ingrained, then the group changes the weekly challenge.

We also keep statistics on who is delivering and how often. These weekly stats should be presented to the group regularly (I recommend every 4 weeks). This promotes accountability.

Having analysed data specific to sports teams, we also now know that when the group successfully achieves these weekly key deliverables, they win the game 90% of the time. This again demonstrates that the best teams have a wealth of active leaders.

Emerging Leader Support Exercise

Gather a list of key people throughout the organisation and allocate them evenly to all leaders in the group. If you are a large organisation then each leader should have five key people in their support group. If you are a smaller organisation then one or two will do. The only requirement is that they cannot choose or be allocated their direct reports and close friends. The idea is to pair them with people in the organisation that they don't know very well. We want to cross-pollinate relationships far and wide.

This whole exercise should take no more than 25 minutes to set up and activate. Upon conclusion each leader's group will have roughly the same amount of people in it. Also, make sure that the younger, less experienced leaders are given younger and less experienced team members in their group.

Now that each leader has an allocated support group, it is important to write down the name of each member of their support group – they will oversee these members for 5 weeks. At this point, they must assess, in their mind's eye, how they would currently rate their relationship with that person out of 10 (1 being poor and 10 being excellent). They then decide where they would like to take that relationship over the course of the program.

This exercise is about building more authentic relationships. In all of the premierships that I've been involved in, the teams that consistently win have this united, family feeling. This evolves from trust. In these winning teams there is a greater level of mutual trust than I see from the teams that aren't getting success. To build this trust you need to first invest in each other emotionally. If you've never taken the time to get to know someone, then how can they truly trust you, and how can you trust them? All leaders will be given the challenge to get to know their support group and it leads to a breaking of any unresolved issues that may be lingering.

The aim is to build a culture that is caring. This can be a challenging exercise for a lot of people, but as the weeks go on it becomes easier and easier.

> 'No one cares how much you know, until they know how much you care.'

Community Leadership Initiative Exercise

This is an exercise that helps good leaders become great leaders. Sporting clubs and boardrooms are a great place to acquire leadership skills, and these skills should be taken and applied practically within the community. The leadership group should get together and discuss how they can best utilise their leadership skills out in the community. This should be an ongoing and regular commitment for the duration of the season (or in a corporate environment, for the duration of the program).

There are many ways that the leadership group can take their skills to the community. The following are examples of what teams have done:

- Raising money for a charity.
- Volunteering time to improve the community in some way.

- Washing cars at the local CFA to raise money.
- Helping a family or community service provider in need with household chores.
- Working in a soup kitchen to feed the less fortunate.

Whatever the community initiative chosen, it's solely about improving and giving back to the community – nothing else. There are many different ways to take leadership into the community. You can work with the elderly, the disadvantaged, or the homeless. There are literally thousands of options available that will demonstrate leadership and care, and it should not be hard for the team to come up with an appropriate initiative.

Share The Chair Exercise

In this exercise the leadership facilitator needs to step back and relinquish the chairing of the meeting to the rest of the group. The purpose of this exercise is to remove dependence and create self-sufficient, strong leaders who are capable of taking control, directing the team, and achieving a sense of personal accomplishment. The team member chairing the meeting is encouraged to invest their time, prepare, and take ownership of the meeting. This promotes personal growth and a sense of achievement, and it also challenges the emerging leader to step outside of their comfort zone.

During each meeting, the leaders should take turns in chairing, and in taking, preparing and distributing the meeting minutes. The team member responsible for the meeting minutes must commit to sending them to the group within 48 hours of the meeting.

The leader who is taking the minutes will then be responsible for chairing the following week's meeting.

While the facilitator takes a back seat, they are still very much in control, and they are responsible for ensuring that all of the weekly program requirements are managed and completed at every stage.

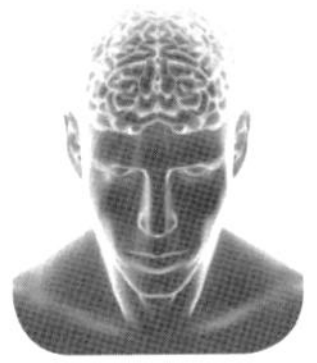

CHAPTER 2

From Surviving to Thriving as a Team

Every living system on our precious planet is an eloquent expression of the universe's astonishing ability to come into perfect balance and then to do what life is meant to do, to thrive. Like every living thing, we are designed to thrive, and yet for so many individuals and teams in the workplace, the reality is that it's more about surviving than thriving, just trying to hang on and doing what's required to get by.

Is this really the best we can do? We have been evolving for 250,000 generations, only to emerge as people that can at times be an enemy to growth and life itself. We can do better. It's time we started to seriously look at how we operate as a species and figure out how we can evolve in to team players. Starting with our work environment, as this is where we spend the majority of our time.

Winning Culture

The first thing that needs to be discussed before I get into the actual methodology of how to create a winning team culture; is to actually define the term itself. To begin, I must first define what culture is. Culture is about one united group with the same positive mindset owning and working towards the same winning vision with clear boundaries and effective behaviours.

A winning culture is all about buying into and owning a shared vision in the team that will ultimately result in success. Once the vision is set (and then owned) the group energy will reflect this, and when a newcomer enters the organisation, the sense of culture is truly sensed.

In a recent Gallup poll from 2013, it was revealed that around 70% of Australians feel disengaged at work. Australia has one of the highest disengagement rates in the world, and this is alarming. Particularly considering we are 'the lucky country'!

In the sporting and business arenas I consider this a huge challenge. The methodology discussed in this book is about creating a winning culture by advancing the people that are already in the organisation. By exploring and discovering ways to keep people engaged as a team, we are actively involving the group, encouraging ownership, and promoting a fun, active and mutually rewarding environment. For management, we are encouraging tenure, reducing recruitment requirements, and maximising performance. All winners when it comes to financial outlay. In Australia, recruiting costs are running at approximately 1.5 times annual salary, so the ability to engage and retain valuable team members has a dynamite impact on an organisation's bottom-line. Where as, according to the 2013 Aon Hewitt survey, the costs incurred when investing in traditional engagement strategies (e.g. Reward & Recognition) have a 100% return on investment. The results speak for themselves, and with a new and innovative program, these results are exceeded in spades.

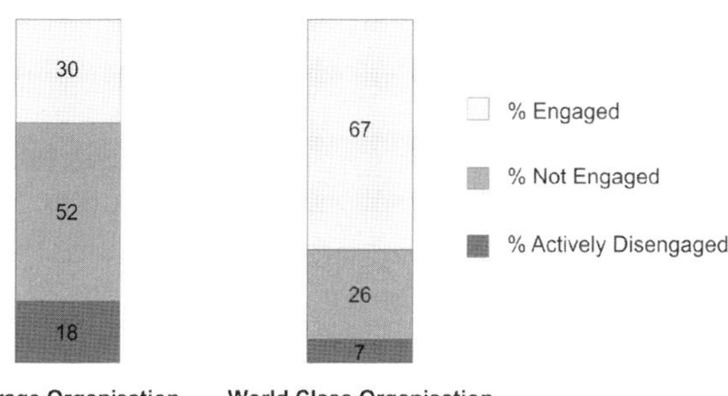

- **The Engaged Employee** – Works with a passion and feels a profound connection to the organisation they work for. They drive innovation and move the organisation forwards.
- **The Non-engaged Employee** – Is essentially there in body only. They're sleep walking through their day. Marking time, but not energy or passion, into their work.
- **The Actively Disengaged Employee** – Isn't just unhappy at work; they're busy acting out their unhappiness. Every day these workers undermine the efforts of their engaged co-workers

Be Brutally Honest: What is it really like in your work place?

In today's business sector, employee engagement and loyalty are more vital than ever before to an organisation's success and competitive edge. Almost 70% of all disengaged employees would change employers right now for as little as a 5% pay increase. Engaged employees on the other hand, would need at least a 20% increase to consider the same switch.

So a winning culture must start by maximising your engagement levels. When this occurs, more leaders emerge and you are well on your way to building a dynamic winning culture.

'Some people say culture is the immune system of the winning team.'

It can be defined as the collective programming of the minds, characterising members of one team from others. It can also be seen as the development or improvement of the mind through education or training. Throughout my years working with over 100 teams in numerous roles in sport and in business, it's abundantly clear that there's a strong distinction that sets apart organisations and teams that have sustainable success from those that don't. This undoubtedly starts with engagement, which creates new leadership and triggers a thriving culture.

Sustainable Success

Within a winning culture you find respect, trust and easy living. You know you have a thriving culture when your existing team members talk about their team and its positive culture with their friends and family. These people then become your extended cheerleading squad! If you have a look at the most successful teams, those who enjoy sustainable success also have a solid and authentic leadership ethos. Additionally, this ethos is so engrained into the fabric of the team at all levels, that when new recruits come in, there's an immediate comprehension of the expectations that must be adhered to. They are surrounded by it, and they see it everywhere they turn.

Former captain and coach of the Australian National Hockey Team, the Kookaburras, Dr Ric Charlesworth says, 'The best teams have a critical mass of leaders.' This is the key to sustainable success. A winning culture transforms somewhat-engaged team members into fully engaged leaders.

Organisations live and die by the people they employ and their volunteers – no matter what industry or code. If you get it wrong you can send the organisation back years. If you don't have a strong culture in place when a storm arrives, then chances are you'll soon regress and find yourselves in another rebuilding phase. If this happens, attracting new recruits will be harder than ever, while the demoralising effect it will have on your current team members will prompt them to entertain the idea of exploring greener pastures.

Team Member Retention[2]

In both business and sport, team member retention has a vital influence on your return on investment. Losing key players and staff members because of fading morale and disengagement is a waste of cash – period. In general, people don't leave companies; they leave their leaders. Leaders lay the foundation for allegiance, and also too often disloyalty.

If you reflect on your past employment history, assessing what the critical components were that prompted your departure, you will usually notice a pattern and the message is clear; there were issues with the leadership. Most people don't change jobs solely based on money. They almost never resign spontaneously or without careful consideration. Something at some point made it wrong. And if you do some digging, you will find that it's not the company they blame;

2. The sentiment of the story was taken from this article www.huffingtonpost.com/greg-savage/people-dont-leave-companies

it's not the team; it's not the office layout and it's not the location; in fact, in almost all cases, it's the leadership.

They joined the organisation because they thought it was right for them at the time, and they desperately wanted it to be right. But when they talk about morale; when they express frustration at the lack of clarity with regard to their career progression; when they say communication is poor; they are telling you that it's the leaders they are leaving. At the end of the day, the leaders and the management team are responsible for the culture, which encompasses morale, communication, progression and personal satisfaction.

When conducting exit interviews, the management team will rarely lay any fault on themselves. They will always question what was wrong with the departing employee, whether they were the right fit for the organisation in the first place, and whether they are leaving to chase more money. A business is just people and machines. No one resigns because of that. It's the culture, the motivation, the behaviours, the environment, the encouragement, the vision, the learning and development, and the direction set by the leaders that they are inspired to follow, or not.

The next time someone resigns, take a moment to reflect on what it actually is that they are resigning from. It's not usually the company they are leaving; it's the leadership.

The main reason people leave or look elsewhere is because they're disengaged. They have withdrawn, they are offering less productivity and they are probably working hard (and not working smart). There's less chance of retaining people if they don't have a vision for themselves, possibly because the organisation doesn't have a clear vision for itself either. A great way to incite a vigorous debate is to start a conversation on organisational culture in a team.

Three Types of People in Every Team

In general, there are three types of people in any organisation or sports team, and these correspond with psychological concepts of adult development, or even the steps to maturity.

The first type, at stage one, is called the singular person. These people are followers, they possess a herd mentality similar to sheep. Everyone in an organisation has experienced this state of being, often at the beginning of his or her tenure. When you introduce a new recruit or team member, they usually begin as sheep. They begin by modelling themselves on others in the group so they can quickly assimilate and fit in with the group.

These singular people definitely want to integrate, and they rely heavily on authority. They don't yet know where they fit into the jungle precisely, but what they are quick to do is to mirror other people around them. In most cases, they end up replicating the behaviours of someone who is at the second stage of development – the individual.

The individual is also referred to as the *'me person'*. A typical example of this second stage of maturity is when you have a young player who has developed over time and has now secured his spot on the field. In AFL terminology, we say he's managed to hold down his position on the wing. This player has now made connections and found some significance within the team. He's going to do whatever it takes to hold on to that position, because he's experiencing these positive new sensations and he is now becoming an official and contributing member of the team. This is a good thing; we need him to concentrate on improving his craft and maintaining his position on the wing. This player is a critical component of the team's success. On the other hand, from a coaching perspective, we don't want him to stay there too long because he needs to progress to the next level of maturity, or mental stage. This is the real team player, what many call the 'we person'.

The *we people* are the true leaders of a championship winning team. The *we people* really see the bigger picture and they understand the power of unity and equality. These people are interdependent and long-term thinkers. They are authentic, respected, and they lead by example. They have gone through the mental stages of the singular and the individual, and are now firmly entrenched in the team-player mental stage. They will, however, sometimes drop back into individual mode, which is okay, so long as they end up back in the team-player category the majority of the time. This is another reason why it's important to have a wealth of *we people* in the organisation, you need others to take over and pick up the slack when a leader reverts back to the *me person* mode for a while. If there are more team players, then the ones who are modelling behaviour (because they are still in the singular phase) will have no choice but to emulate the *we people*, which is great! If there are not enough team players on the team however, then the singular people will end up modelling the individualists, and this will be to the teams' detriment.

This is the trick to sustainable success. If you have a critical mass of me players in the organisation, then at best, success is short lived. These people are only resourceful for a short period, because they're all about themselves. They're typically ego driven, and very much about looking after number one. The key thing to understand here is that when the pressure is applied, usually in other big games or when sales are down, it's generally the *me people* that let everyone else down and crack. They're the ones that will go missing, complain, blame others or just won't show up on the day when the big game needs to be played.

In my leadership program, no matter where I'm coaching, I aim for a simple, easy to understand model that works well with teams from any background. The trick is to fast track as many people in to the we category as is possible. It is these *we people* that manage and thrive in high-pressure situations.

The next stage is to encourage the team players to work on moulding and nurturing the culture in the right direction. The *we person* needs to benchmark the behaviours required to become a solid leader; it's up to the *we people* in the group to bring the *me people* up to their level.

At the beginning of any coaching program, it's very important to take stock of the number of people you have, and what groups they fall into. It's then equally important to educate your team on this model. It then becomes much easier for them to realise who's holding them back. This jumpstarts growth, and the team are usually elevated quickly. So basically it's about educating and re-educating the *me people* and encouraging them to become *we people*, because they are critical for quick, long-term, sustainable success. Every person has a role to play in the team's success. The best players understand and know their individual role within the team, and this creates flow. When the flow kicks in, the team can handle vast amounts of pressure. All leading stakeholders in a team, whether it be the head coach, the general manager or the CEO, play a critical role in the success of a team. If they are a *me person*, it's unlikely the team will be able reach its full potential. Even though these key stakeholders are critical to an organisation's success and culture, it's the day to day people in the broader team that are largely responsible for the creation of really long-term success in the organisation. There's no question that the people in senior management positions have a critical role to play, however, if you've got a critical mass of *we people* in the team, it won't matter if a coach, senior management, or even the CEO departs the organisation, you will still find that the team is more than likely to thrive no matter who replaces them.

Of course, you should always strive to make sure the replacement is a we person. Over time stats have revealed that the average length of an AFL head coach's career is only 3.3 years, so you want to attain maximum impact in a minimal time frame with the right person. Think 'waterfall effect'. It starts from the top, and flows down from there.

Most of the lessons I've learnt about leadership in my time have been from bad coaches or bad bosses, who through their example taught me what not to do. I think that all told, only around 10% of my past bosses and coaches were actually great leaders. This is pretty poor, but it is also likely to be a fair representation of what the broader public feels upon reflection.

Creating a Critical Mass of 'We Players'

To establish the right players quickly, the coach or team leader needs to be a we person – first and foremost. Secondly, if there is a leadership group in the team, then they have to develop a firm understanding of the three different types of people, and the mental stages they move through. From there, the leadership group needs to work together to become fully united in their approach, going outside of themselves in all dimensions to build trust amongst their peers.

Another thing that needs to be understood is that it's all about equality. Once the leadership team have grasped the concept that everyone is equal and that they are there to serve, then they have to walk the walk and serve first and foremost. Then team unity will kick in. If the leaders are in it for themselves, for their own satisfaction, or for their own personal journey, then it needs to be addressed, or a thriving culture will not flow.

Equality = Unity = Truth

When you focus on understanding equality, earning the trust and respect of your peers is not as difficult as it may initially seem. Earning trust must begin within the leadership team. Adequate time and effort must first be invested in the formation of the leadership team; getting them working as a highly skilled cohesive unit. Once this is achieved, the leadership team needs to identify the cliques within the organisation. By 'cliques' I mean the separate groups within the group. As a leader it's important to understand that people are more likely to like you if you are like them. So it's now time to blend in, empathise and become the chameleon!

> 'People are more likely to like you, if you are like them.'

When there is a clear understanding of behaviours and a clear understanding of what's acceptable and what's not, some people might still decide to break the agreement and behave in a different way. But if the team tackles this problem as a group, to show unity and equality, then these issues can be resolved successfully and quickly.

An Ethos of Trust

The whole organisation should understand that the ethos and the culture of a winning teams' success is based around trust. If everyone prioritises and reciprocates mutual trust, and is focused on serving others, then the creation of a *we people* environment is fast-tracked. Another critical element is to ensure buy in from the support staff and the senior managers. They need to be on the same page also, and if they are all stuck in the *me* mental stage, then the whole flow of the organisation will be substandard and compromised. In other words, the cultural flow will be slower and weaker.

'Success does not lie.'

The quickest way to achieve sustainable success – apart from spending up large on recruiting direct talent for short-term gain – is to create a *we* organisation based on trust, understanding and selflessness. Once the leadership team have an understanding of their role, they can go about bringing the *me people* into the *we* category. This is a designed approach that takes skill, precision and planning, because when you're targeting the *me person*, these people can be highly sensitive. Usually, the ones that don't handle pressure well also think that they are extremely valuable. At times players and employees can overestimate their value and form an unhealthy level of self-confidence – manifesting as an overbearing ego. This often creates resistance, and this type of person cracks quickly under pressure, especially if they believe they are special in some way.

Keeping Your Finger on the Pulse

Building a winning team within any organisation requires a great deal of precision, understanding and empathy when dealing with people. That's why all coaches and team leaders – at all levels – must keep their heads in the game at all times, and not in the sand.

One of the biggest issues that can be on an elite sports persons mind is money. They have a short time to make it, and they want to make as much as they can as quickly as possible! Basically, they want to know what's in it for them. This thought is constantly running through their mind.

I know of a team who recruited a key icon. The leaders were all asked to take a pay cut to get this new, so-called star recruit on board. The leaders obliged and trusted the team's management were making the right choice for the overall success of the team. Once the new recruit arrived, he was naturally welcomed with open arms by all team members. The leaders went outside themselves to ensure the prize recruit was given every possible avenue to succeed. They knew the recruit would behave in the sheep mentality for a few months, but with natural progression and with the leaders' guidance, they expected the new recruit to quickly evolve through the three levels. Six months in, and the recruit was not only all about himself, he was not mentally capable of fitting in – both on and off the field. Very soon the recruit was removed from the team. The leaders then lost trust with the management for compromising their contract sizes and not signing like-minded people. Two years down the track and the team was no further advanced. The leaders also knew that the window of opportunity to achieve their ultimate dream was rapidly closing due to their age, and this only added fuel to their internal raging fire. Yes, you could say that the recruiters and management simply got one wrong, but in the elite sports industry every bad choice like this has a flow-on effect that affects many team members and it can have a negative flow on effect that will impact the success of the group for many years in some cases.

To ensure a thriving organisation, it's about building the *we people* culture, and to do this everyone needs to be treated as an equal, and understood completely. A successful culture should be guarded and protected fiercely, and a new recruit's ability to successfully assimilate and become a we person should be paramount, even prioritised over natural ability. Some organisations call it a 'no dickhead policy'!

There will almost always be discrepancies with individual salaries, however, if a business is paying big dollars for a new recruit, its paramount they ensure the person has the desire and the ability to become we quickly.

Understanding the WE Methodology

Another critical component is understanding the *we* methodology, and the reasons behind it thoroughly. To create winning team success, teams need to see the bigger picture. That is, if we recruit players who are strong minded *me* people then that's great; they're probably going to get a few more members in the gates because they're the big icons of the game, but whatever you do, educate them on the *we* mentality the minute they walk through the door. Then it's their call how they behave, it's their choice. But they need to know the choices first and foremost; with that, I mean boundaries.

If they're not able to understand the *we* mentality they'll have a short career, and so will your team. In this book, I'll take you through a system that I've used in many organisations throughout Australia. This can be easily implemented, and will actually allow you to further systematise your organisation's methodology with the *we, me* and singular people model.

This model is now being used successfully in all business sectors, in elite sporting clubs, right down through to semi-professional and regional community sports teams in a number of codes of sport.

Answering the Why

The question I always get from clients when looking for assistance is, 'Why bother building culture when people don't hang around long enough?' The answer to that question is another question: 'Why aren't the people in the organisation hanging around long enough?' When organisations start digging for the reasons, they usually find out that it's because their people are not happy or enjoying themselves; they're not engaged.

The key is to set things up so that there will always be a leadership pipeline plan in place. This is what the best teams do and although they still play a significant role in success, it doesn't matter who the coach is. At the end of the day, the coach or CEO might want to disappear, or may get recruited by another organisation. So it is critical you make sure the people are running the show (within reason) when it comes to culture.

Another question I get asked often is 'What if the coach or the CEO is a *me* person? How do we educate them on the *WE* methodology?' My answer to that is to ask them why they got a coach or a CEO with the *me* attitude. Usually the horse has already bolted before I'm able to get this information across to my organisations. But the key thing here is education.

Traits of a typical *me* person: always showing up late and leaving early; stays close to their own clique and doesn't want to mingle; regularly complaining about anything and everything; never going above and beyond for anyone unless they are pushed to; it's always someone's else's fault; moody; unpredictable; goes missing when the pressure is on; rarely invests in or enquires about others;

rarely buying a shout of drinks at the bar for others; the list goes on and on.

Stepping Back When It's Time

For a manager or coach to get the most out of their team, and to work smart instead of hard, they must have a plan and a strategy from the get go. This includes knowing the following three important stages of team success. The end goal is to be able to step back when the time is right, allowing others to lead the charge.

There are three key components to building a sound skyscraper:

1. The foundation or the formwork needs to be rock solid.
2. Then the framework or brickwork can be applied.
3. The scaffolding is then set up to hold up the next stages of the development.

If this is not done in the right order, then when pressure is applied, it will not last the test of time.

The same goes for any developing organisation:

1. The leadership and culture ethos is the foundation, and it needs to be rock solid.
2. The managers and coaches set up the team structures and systems.
3. The leaders and all team members play their own important individual role, progressing one level at a time.

A great coach basically sets up the scaffolding for the team at level one – preparing them to progress to level two. Once the team moves to level two, the coach then sets up the scaffolding to progress to levels 3, 4 and 5. A great coach just places the scaffolding around the team. It's the team that lays the bricks themselves. The coach is responsible for putting a strong support structure in place in alliance with the direction the organisation is taking. The team itself is the energy behind this structure. They're the ones that need to work together to determine where the next bricks are to be placed. The team members are the ones that must keep each other in line. In doing so, we find that when we get to the top of the building, it can handle any amount of pressure. When the winds come in, the winning team stands strong, unwavered, and can handle any storm.

When you reach the top, the scaffolding is no longer required, and the coach has done his or her job. At this point the players should possess the understanding, knowledge and knowhow of what's required culturally according to the broader plan. The team built the skyscraper so they know its strengths and weaknesses, and this creates a unified equal approach to premiership success. The same applies to any business.

Get Out Of Your Own Way

On the sports field, and in particular in the AFL, assistant coaches are required to meet with their smaller teams at the main breaks throughout the game. They need to motivate and inspire, assessing areas of strength and weakness from the previous play. They have their small group's attention for roughly five minutes at each break. This is an extremely brief window of opportunity to pass on the many messages required to achieve maximum impact.

All too often I see and hear coaches trying in vain to solve their group's problems, instructing the team on the things they need to do and change. This is done both for each individual and for the collective. Most of the time these demands are not being received at all. The athlete's mind is already in overdrive, which means it's full. The athlete is also dealing with themselves and their own inner critic.

The alternative to this, especially if the coach wants to achieve a far greater impact with these five minute windows, is to educate the group on how to independently problem-solve in the heat of battle. This needs to start at training. The coach should encourage the group to self-assess and take 100% ownership of their current situation. This takes practise.

The coach should commence the five-minute game breaks by imparting a few relevant key statistics from the game thus far. Then pass it over to the players in the group to assess, discuss and debate, before agreeing on the way forward. Most coaches I see today get themselves in the way and they behave like preachers and dictators with their message. Get out of the way! This old school coaching methodology has been passed on from when these coaches were playing the game, but the game has changed. If you want to keep up, then step back and empower your teams to lead the charge. We don't learn when we are being told; we learn when we are empowered and when experiences are based on our own decisions and consequences. At its core, the coach is managing; not leading. This again mirrors the role of the manager in the business world. Lead your team! The best coaches also know how to trigger their individual team members when it comes to the seven key neurological motivators, which are pain, pleasure, reward, recognition, self improvement, self direction and transcendent purpose. Through these, coaches can maximise their message and time; this is working smart, not hard.

The Body of an Organisation

Two vital requirements in order for any team and organisation to thrive are:

- Quality *systems, processors and game plans*, which I call 'the brain' of the organisation.
- Quality *leadership, engagement and culture*, which I call 'the heart' of the organisation.

The two most important organs of the body are the brain and the heart, and we cannot survive without them functioning. When all 4 major valves of the heart are pumping well, there is more oxygen pumping to the brain, and it's getting there far quicker than if you had only 1 valve (or a fraction of 1 valve) functioning, which I liken to most organisations that are just surviving.

In other words, the brain will work on small portions of blood flow, but it will be working harder than it should be, and it's not sustainable long term. When unexpected additional pressure is applied, the body will often break down. If you have an unlimited amount of blood flow, full of fresh oxygen, the brain will then work at full capacity, and it will be better equipped if there are problems. This creates a vibrant, energetic and healthy body (or organisation)!

Empowerment and Ownership Exercise – Presenting Leadership Initiatives

Another effective exercise is for each team member to present a *leadership initiative* to the group when it comes to best practice in leadership, culture, team building and engagement. This can be done through video, audio, a media clipping or an article, depending on what works for the presenter.

(On my websites you can find a database of articles and other links that can be a good starting point: www.premiershipcoach.com.au and www.engageandgrow.com.au)

The purpose of this exercise is for the leaders to share relevant information that they feel would be interesting and useful for the team at the current stage they find themselves at. These short presentations should run for 5-10 minutes, so it needs to be brief, and there needs to be time to generate some meaningful discussion.

Once the leaders are presenting ideas on how to create a dynamic culture, they will start owning the outcomes and the direction of the team more than ever. It also gives people a voice, allowing them to sharpen their leadership and presenting skills in front of the group.

This should be done weekly until all leaders have completed the task.

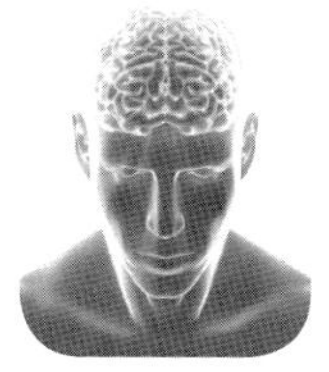

CHAPTER 3

It's All About The Mind

Challenges of an Elite Mind

One of the more serious dilemmas that surface for elite athletes and business leaders is how able (both physically and mentally) they are to cope with mounting tasks and responsibilities. This topic can be controversial, because training in sports is tied in with a lot of personal development as well. Athletes are often dealing with gruelling physical training requirements, as well as a vast amount of psychological and mental work.

Visualisation and meditation are two popular techniques used currently to assist leaders in evolving their mental acumen. While visualisation and meditation have their place, and are important pieces of the jigsaw puzzle, the most critical factor in ensuring you are at your best mentally, is to continually empty your mind of all extraneous and unresourceful thought patterns that plague it. If the mental emotional cup is overflowing, then when pressure is applied, a mental collapse (be it major or minor) is imminent. This can cause an emotional outburst, or in some cases on the sports field, a physical breakdown or injury of some description. No amount of visualisation and meditation can prevent this.

Elite sports teams are putting far too much emphasis and focus on developing the athlete's physical competencies, and failing to invest adequate resources into the development and advancement of the athlete's mind. The tide is however starting to turn. We regularly witness elite athletes in the headlines for all the wrong reasons. The system is built on heralding heroes, but what goes up must come down. We just don't focus enough on keeping our athletes balanced and ahead of the game mentally. Subsequently, a large proportion of elite athletes will continue to psychologically crash, or continue to not reach the lofty heights they once dreamed of because their mental foundation is built on unstable clay footings.

This is one of the key points that this book explores in great detail. It is a crucial element in winning team success, and I will cover this in more detail as you read on.

> **'There must be a mutual 50/50 balance between body and mind to thrive.'**

A common misperception with regard to elite leaders and performers is that their performance is based solely on what they DO physically. In reality, elite sport and outstanding leadership is not possible without strong, mental strength and focus as well. Precisely what this mental strength is, and how to tap into it has been the subject of much discussion, but in recent years, the area of sports technology has been keeping abreast with the more advanced levels of overall fitness. No longer is it simply about practising as much as possible. Players now need to train both the body and, even more importantly, the brain.

In many of the sporting teams I've worked with there is a clear and urgent need for a corresponding upgrade of mental sharpness to balance off physical prowess. A professionally applied acuity of mind goes beyond emotional weaknesses, which means that it has the ability to be open wide, mental vents to accommodate extra pressure whenever the application is needed.

When the mind is not suitably prepared for the endurance levels that the body has been trained for, then whenever pressure is applied, but not accepted, there is a stuttering that occurs between the engine, the mind, and the fluid transmission into the body action.

In sport, the resultant features are forms of mental straying, such as ineptness in fielding the ball, not reading the play correctly, inaccuracy in kicking and a loss of energy. The list is a lot longer than that.

When mental weaknesses are not remedied in any field, interaction between mind and body starts to break down, not unlike a couple in a relationship that gets involved in nagging and justification. Unless rearranged quickly into harmony, the synchronisation so vital in play lacks rhythm and coordination.

The Irrational Mind and The Pharmaceutical Band Aid

Within the conditioned ego of each mental system, there are many unresolved areas of shyness. These *lack of confidence* areas are like potholes in a road that require filling and levelling if the human carriage is to roll forward smoothly on the journey of life. Problems arise for the ego when the mind runs across a rut that signifies – by some sort of shock – that there is repair work to be done. Most ruts or holes in causeways are caused where incorrect material has been used as subsurface bedding.

People who want their holes filled up before they have cleaned them out invariably turn to cheap products or quick fixes. It is indisputable that drugs can fill holes temporarily; but it is a lie to suggest that they can resolve a problem. They can, at best, allay or arrest the disturbance. Come off the drugs and the same problem still manifests. The problem is not the cause or the residual issue.

While the drugs applicable to sports teams might be unrelated to the various substances that people abuse their bodies with on a day-to-day basis in other fields, all drugs react with us in the same way. They can create a dependence cycle that is difficult – if not impossible – to get out of alone.

The real issue is pain, and that is what substances and addictions are used to mask. This pain is internal. It resides in the areas of the brain that Sigmund Freud described as *the unconscious* or *the id*. The problem comes from an issue that has not been resolved. Because the rational mind refuses to accept responsibility for the issue, there is the creation of a problem. The problem is the manifested issue. If it is not resolved then it becomes an aberration. It will demand an audience. The demand can manifest in an accident or an illness. Or it can become an emotional backlash or backwash.

Emotions are feelings that have never been grounded. Like beliefs, they have never formed from foundation. Emotions are like the frothy bits on the surface waves of the sea: a series of peaks and troughs; a never-ending series of broken promises. When we have the courage to clean out our holes of the slurry of emotional teasing and beliefs, then we are in a position to lay down a solid foundation. To attempt to fill the holes is an exercise in futility. Drugs therefore have limited capabilities and should be used only as a means to calm the situation. They should not be seen as a solution to mental disturbance.

Only those who have the courage and the wish to live freely will become excited in developing methods of mind release outside the practices of a world dominated by drug addiction. The rest will never be more than groups of sheep penned in by a society, manipulated by drug companies and herded by the sheep dogs known as the medical profession.

Drug addiction takes many forms. The main one we are concerned with here is how athletes will sometimes cheat to fill the gaps in their knowledge and strength.

Why People Crack Under Pressure

The problem areas in mind and body – the ones that do not respond to heightened game pressure – are in the main mechanistic movements that have been instilled from outside sources. They do not resonate with natural talent.

If untreated, the next crack in the physical system is a mental giving way that results in uncapped amounts of body injury. The warning signs are always evident to those who are skilled at reading the character plays of oncoming weaknesses. The importance of prevention of an overload of stress cannot be underestimated. Unless resolved, the wounded and maimed will eventually surmount the numbers of fit and able.

When a red light flashes on the dashboard of the car, those of sane mind stop the engine and inquire as to what problems there may be. When will management learn to read the warning signs and address a full mental preparation of their performers? This is a necessity so that all players (particularly the younger ones) can absorb the required toughness to perform at their top-level week-after-week without injury.

This is a short simple laying out of mechanistic features that dog the development of future performers and leaders in every professional sport and in business.

'People who are precious simply cannot handle pressure.'

The Collapsing Mind of the Athlete

Team players who are skilful and ruthlessly competitive are on every recruiter's list when it comes to selecting any team. However, all too often new athletes are wide-eyed and energised, then within a short amount of time pressure mounts and a slight or major mental collapse is imminent. The collapse may be as severe as it was for me when I was coming through the elite ranks as a 19-year-old, or it may just be a run of minor setbacks, such as nursing hamstring, ankle or shoulder injuries.

Isn't it interesting that in today's sporting landscape, athlete injuries are by far the biggest issue teams are facing on the road to success?

As they say, the body is led by the mind.

Whether it be demanding coaches, mega contracts, persistent parents who offer self-obsessed advice, team supporters blogging daily or the hungry media seeking another headline, it's all useless pressure if not managed.

Next comes the internal abuse, followed by the fear of making mistakes in the arena, then the fear of not fitting in, and very soon the *singular athlete* has arrived and is trapped, or somewhat blocked, temporarily or indefinitely.

Experts are then called in and go about trying to rebuild and restructure the athlete's self-belief and confidence over and over again. It's like going down to the beach with a bucket and spade on a cloudy day and building sand castles on the edge of the water: as fast as you build them, the waves are going to break them straight back down again.

So what is happening is our athletes have not built (or are not being taught to build) a strong mental foundation. If we compare these athletes to racehorses, they are like colts. They come out as two-year-olds and all they know to do is to run. However, when they come out into senior company, or onto the big stage, they haven't got the background or the strength of a solid mental foundation to work from. The road to team and individual success will now take many more twists and turns than first anticipated because the mental road has developed too many potholes that were temporarily patched up and previously filled in with sub-standard material that has now eroded away. The only sustainable solution is to dig the entire road back up with a new sound and solid foundation that will not falter under any amount of traffic.

Self-Belief Only Causes Grief

To reach full potential an elite performer must first eliminate all *beliefs*.

Everything in the world that we are living in right now is altering. It is speeding up, and the only way our athletes and teams are going to stay at the top of the tree is to make damn sure that the roots are solid and sound. Ever known of a tree that could survive with a set of rotten roots? The thing is, it's in the mind – that's where the breakdown is, and it goes back to *belief*. Belief is no longer valid. It never was valid, but in the old days people got away with believing in hope, faith, trust and all of that kind of stuff. It doesn't work anymore. Even the old story that 'one must have loyalty to the firm as the firm will give loyalty back to you.' The same thing is said in the sporting environment. 'Athletes played for the club and the club was loyal to the athlete.' Where have those days gone? They got left behind over 10 years ago. What I'm saying is that carrying beliefs is also old hat and needs to be left behind with loyalty if you want to reach your full potential as an athlete, and in life in general.

The new ball game is in the intelligence of the person that's pulling on the footy boots, the Speedos, the running shoes, etc. If the athlete's mental foundation is solid then the athlete *knows* what they are capable of, and they *know* they can repeat it. When this is the case you have a seasoned individual team player.

A great team runs on foundation; it does not run on ego or singular thinking. Know your role; know your capabilities and the structures. That's it. The elite player has all the skills they need. Now it is time to release the mind by removing old belief systems.

This is where the mind can do what it knows best; that is, compete in automatic mode. But automatic mode flows best when the athlete is clear in the mind Monday-through-Sunday. As soon as the athlete feels the need to build on *self-belief* they are blocking natural raw energy, which means they will not reach their potential. Self-belief is a man-made belief and it does not come from foundation. It is simply an illusion. It can work as a starting point to get going, just like a starter motor, but when you are amongst elite company it will only lead to disappointment.

Lastly, too many players these days are too scared to tell the coach that they are lacking confidence because, unbeknown to them, the mind is built on flimsy and false pretences. So they continually fight an internal battle in their journey, hoping to stumble across confidence again. Confidence only seems to work when fear of future failure is safely put to bed. So the first place to start when lacking confidence is to go back to competence. This then takes the athlete back to knowing clearly what they are capable of, and competent at, and what their role is. Then, they can simply stick to it. The mind knows what to do if you allow it to be free of beliefs. Self-belief is a form of self-hypnosis – nothing more.

The 'Rough Diamond' Elite Athlete

What kind of players are coaches and recruiters looking for? It's a question that always arises. In the sporting arena they call these players the 'rough diamonds'.

In other words, the difference between them and the super elite athletes, as I wish to call them, is simply that they've got all the requirements, but they have lost their way mentally on the journey to fulfill their dreams. So, if you like, the quantity is inside them, but the quality is not being found because they're not being polished and maintained. It's just the same as a diamond!

A rough diamond comes out of the ground and looks like nothing special, but once they start to wash it and polish it, shine it and all the rest of it, then what you've got is a rare diamond.

For a team to flow and reach their full potential, the coaches need to take the pressure off the super athletes and they need to put more pressure on the rough diamonds to polish their attributes. With that you get a dynamic team. I can't see that happening while many teams continue to pay a huge amount of money towards the so-called super athletes and keep the rough diamonds on a low scale pay rate. So there's got to be an incentive for the rough diamonds to go about polishing themselves.

'The rough diamonds are not given the latest tools to polish themselves down!'

It's important to have the right administration, coaches, trainers, physiotherapists and mind strategists on the team. If these people have the skills and are team players in all respects, then they're going to turn out quality players. Adversely, if they don't have the skills, then the up and comers are not going to learn what's appropriate.

I'm concerned that some of the mind-training that is currently being taught to young sports people is not going to help them. You've got to develop a complete understanding of the players' lives. Unfortunately, you hear about certain athletes and players in the media when they do something stupid, such as getting into a fight, getting charged with assault, drink driving, and so on. Everybody wrings their hands and says these things should never have happened, but that's not good enough! What you've got to do is train that problem out of the person when they first arrive at the club.

A lot of people have bad things to say about players who get in trouble, but I say that they are nothing more than the products of financial backers who just buy in who they want and drop kick who they don't with impunity. These financiers have no interest whatsoever in the whole picture and do not intend to ever build up the player's character. This is especially prevalent in the NFL in the United States of America.

When new players come into a winning team they become part of a family. They become part of a team effort. At the moment, what you're seeing in the elite sporting world is gloss. It doesn't matter which club, it's all gloss and the media supports it all.

What I mean by this, just as an example, is that quite often all the administration wants is glossy material and they have no interest in developing the mental quality of players. All they want is excitement; all they want is the drama so that they can market the player or concept and please their bosses upstairs. When it comes to building a united and powerful team you've got to start looking for these administrators within the organisation and re-educate them with the understanding and the big picture.

'These athletes have not embedded a firm mental foundation.'

Time and time again I see elite teams marketing young athletes purely to get audiences into the stands. At this stage in their development, these athletes have not embedded a firm mental foundation to build from. This means when external mental pressure is increased (due to perceived additional expectations) a mental, and then physical, collapse is imminent. These athletes are much too green to be up in lights. The mind can't handle the pressure from external sources and then the body follows suit and breaks down causing injury, which can vary from a few weeks to multiple seasons. This is a real issue, in my opinion, as the teams are simply not going to get their return on investment with these players, and it's not their fault. The thing is, with this example, it can be quickly rectified with education and understanding.

Move Over Mainstream Psychology: There is a New Way

When coaches and management are going about polishing rough diamonds, the first place they should start is with the recycled stuff they tell players, which they call 'psychology'. This often causes more problems than it fixes. I'm talking about telling people that if they 'believe in themselves hard enough they can be a world leader', and anything else that ridiculous. Players go out onto the field all the time believing that they're going to be successful (you just have to believe) and then they don't succeed. This kind of *believe in yourself* psychology gives you nothing to learn from when you're seeking answers to improve your game.

When you bet on a horse race you take a look at the horses and choose one hoping that it can finish first and win a race. But often enough some horses lead all the way and fall over not far from home, because they don't have the required stamina. They may have the speed, they may have the class, but they lack the inbuilt stamina.

When it comes to athletes, if you can pull these athletes out of the team, then identify the rough diamonds that lack mental stamina and polish them down, you can then create teams that play right up to the final minutes in the last quarter and finish strong – the type of winning team play I'm talking about.

With these rough diamonds it's more or less understanding their history, their DNA, understanding and getting them to understand not what they are but more so who they are.

> 'The rough diamonds need to understand not what they are but who they are!'

To do that you have to have a look at their upbringing, because the DNA is still overloaded or clouded, if you like, by their actual circumstances from childhood through to the present. That's where the core issue comes from. The false belief really doesn't come from their DNA, what really happens is in their upbringing, the old passed-on areas that are in the DNA, are put on demonstration for them to look at in their day-to-day lives.

They can see their inner fears being projected out onto other people. After we have worked with them, they understand that they have to see this as a reflection of themselves. We get them to dig inside themselves, find out what areas they are weak in, and then get them to polish it, muscle it, or whatever you want to do, to bring it up to a standard that matches the other areas we are working. Then you've got the super athlete.

'You can't have a poor opinion about someone else unless you have weakness in you.'

The body and the mind need to be equal in development and strength. These days most elite teams put 90% of their attention into the athlete's physical development. This creates an imbalance, as the body and mind must be equalled, 50/50, to create the super athlete, which in turn delivers a balanced athlete and, subsequently, a balanced team.

The elite super athlete doesn't have weakness. Right now I'm in a whole new field of exploration. It is something that some mind strategists have some idea of, but they can't break through the understanding because they can't get outside of their own ego –

they have all been trained from the same institutional and wage-earning book.

Do you have to burn your ego to be a super athlete? No! But you can't just believe in yourself. You must strip yourself down mentally and then see what parts are working and what parts are not, and clean up the mental area. If you can't get players to do that, it's because the whole platform – their ego – is unstable and shaky.

'When a player is unable to meet the expectations they are walking on thin ice!'

First of all: a clean out is a clean out. Do it right or don't do it at all. If you can't get the person who is covering this crucial area of expertise to fix the athletes they are dealing with, then you've got to give them a kiss goodbye and bring in somebody who knows how to build the appropriate mental foundations. Players need the necessary tools so they can start to clean up and speed up the show.

This kind of stripping down approach works because it's like the old guy that's never been taught to do anything more than use a hammer and a hand saw. You come along with power tools and explain that you would like to have the job done 10 times faster. You show him how to use the power tools. You don't get out a hammer and chisel to deal with an urgent job; you get the latest laser equipment and cut through the deadwood so that you can get to where you want to be.

Players get their energy to work through these issues from within.

The energy's inside; all you've got to do is break through the barriers. Just see it as a potential oil field. You have to go down through the crust to be able to tap into that oil. You've got to go through layers of rock. Then you have to break through the gas field. Then you can tap into the oil – the raw energy. Energy is there, inside everyone's brain. All they have to do is learn how to be able to tap it. And it's not a secret, because I'll tell it to you and I'll tell it to the world. The way that you get there is not by building ideas; the way you get there is by cutting through every obsolete item that the person is carrying in their mental memory. This is similar to the who leadership development style I have spoken about earlier.

Here's another analogy to explain.

It's no different from when you have rust that starts to break through a car's bodywork because it's under the paint job. What do you do? Are you going to paint over it again and pretend that the car's 100%? Or are you going to cut it out and then replace it with good material and then paint it?

There are heaps of analogies. Do you want to have a bogged up car, or do you want to have a car that is clear of rust?

Most people who are resistant to these analogies show clearly that they've been ego-trained. They think that you already have everything you need, and that you've got to keep building on it. A golfer could set a goal of making themselves hit 500 balls in a day, but he might not think when he starts off that he needs to clean up his memory.

What he is probably thinking is that if he hits those 500 balls, then at the end of the day he will be competent enough to hit a 501st ball. The reality is that he might hit it out of bounds, or into a tree, or into the bunkers. He's going to make a mistake even if he's practised 500 shots. Why? Because he doesn't have mental foundation. He has been trained to think that if you hit 500 golf balls, then you can hit every shot from then on in the same way. No! It doesn't happen like that because the moment the pressure goes on in the mind, the mind does a flip and asks, 'Am I up to it?' This all happens subconsciously and, sure enough, the golf hit is not up to it.

It's not about getting rid of that voice, it's about learning to live with it so it doesn't erupt and cause problems at the worst times.

The main problem with the voice for a lot of elite performers in sport and business is that it's mostly silent. It's like a message that arrives in your inbox, but because you haven't turned your computer on yet, you don't know it's in there. You can compare the mind to a computer. If the memory is faulty in your computer, then you can't expect that you're going to get great material when you need to access it quickly.

The Need To Eliminate All Mindsets is Key

We are carrying these subconscious glitches in our minds, and until such time as they make themselves known, we don't know we've got them and we can't do anything about them. The problem is they don't usually make themselves known until it's too late. You find out that your steering is gone and your brakes don't work and you're on angel flight until such time as you can get back on firm ground.

It's like being in a skidding car where you lose complete control. One thing you hopefully learned in driving school is to not touch the brakes! You have to steer into the skid and then come out of it.

> 'Cleaning out all mindsets is imperative for the beginnings of any winning team culture.'

Many trainers are saying that it's enough to be physically fit, and that they already believe their team is mentally tough enough to be the #1 team next year. How many other teams are there saying the same thing?

What they're generally forgetting is that you need to maintain it once you get to a peak. You do this by taking the pressure off. To find out where the tension is and then release it puts you into a cruise mode where you can do what you need to do while conserving as much energy as possible; you only need to put the foot down to steer clear of an obstacle.

At its core, the pressure that creates the shakes stems from the inner and outer ego of the athlete. If given the slightest amount of attention it is clear a mental collapse is imminent. When an athlete has mastered the art of a quiet mind this is where a spring of talent comes to the table. As talent is stored in the memory to be used at will if you know how to unlock it when required. When unlocked the days of getting the yips and the shakes are all but over. This mentality is what makes super elite athletes and champions.

This kind of quiet mind creates champions. This mentality takes training and practice, so adopt the mentality and see if it works for you.

The best way to deal with this is to begin talking to the different clubs and finding out where the rough diamonds are and polish them with urgency. At the moment they don't even know they have a problem because they do not have a trained eye to pick up on it.

This is a fantastic source of untapped ability that can be quickly added to any team. A trained coach (who knows what he is doing) can teach a team how to tap into this mental spring of energy. This is done by working with the individuals and pointing out that they need to dig and (to continue my analogy from before) find out what's under that hard rock and what's under that gas. Then you might have a chance to get that mental energy that leads you to success as a championship-winning team.

If you HAVE energy and NO talent, you will be OK

If you HAVE energy and HAVE talent then you are really lucky,

If you have NO energy but you HAVE talent you could be in a lot of trouble!

– Jeffrey Archer

Team Ethos vs Team Mythos

There is a team mythos (belief) that interferes with the team's ethos. Ethos is what you want. Ethos equals *club spirit*. Mythos interferes with the club spirit. A mythos is unfinished business of periods of season that interferes with the modern program. Mythos creeps into organisations – it's insidious and hangs around like nut grass. You can take the top off the grass on the ground, but the nuts are thriving underneath. It's got to be dug out. Mythos is the underlying system of beliefs.

When a mythos has a strong hold in the organisation, cliques are rampant, a survival mentality is the norm and very soon the club slides down the slippery slope into the abyss. The mythos is held and harboured in the minds of the people in the organisation. As humans we do not bond together; we band together. In other words if a sub group within the team is still stuck in the past with their beliefs then the cultural nut grass is flourishing.

It all starts in the mind; no matter what role you play in the team. It is critical for the athlete to understand that if they cannot get their mental capacity up to the level of their physical strength then they are going to break down throughout the season (in fact many are breaking down before the season). It's important to create a strong team spirit (ethos) by getting the minds of the athletes to enlarge to cope with the extra physical build up. You have to bring the mind and body through together. It's challenging but, just like the physical body, the more the mind is challenged the stronger the mind grows. And because they have not been challenged, their minds have gone into a cesspool, which is rank swamp water. You have to drain the swamp, and then fill it up with nice fresh water.

The next question then is: 'Are you up to it?' 'Who is you?' The you is your mental approach. 'Can it match your physicality?' Very few people make championship level. If you want championship level, you have got to get past the breaker point.

Pressure on players builds from unresolved issues. Nobody has ever been harmed by bringing an issue into the open and dealing with it. If they don't bring it into the open then there is a fear built up in their system. And the more the fear builds up, the more the mind is threatened and then the more they are capable of getting injuries and breaking down mentally. These issues do not have to be sports related, but they do have a habit of interfering with a creditable performance.

To create a strong ethos what we do is bring their minds up to where they are mentally tough, and mentally strong, so that they won't buckle under pressure. The way to clear the pressure is to go through the unresolved issues, because that's the only reason there is pressure – because these problems have never been opened up, put on the table, identified and then cleared. Do that and you're home on a pig's back. You can fool most of the people most of the time, but you cannot fool yourself. If you think you can, then you are heading for a disaster. Get a trained quality mind coach today. These coaches are few and far between, and they do not adhere to and practice current day mainstream institutional teachings.

John 'Sam' Newman quote from the the *Ed & Derm Show* (2014) – Foxtel

> 'The thing that we overlook in my opinion is the fact that most people who have a shot at goal have got no idea what they are trying to do. And we pay lip service to accurate goal kicking when that is the most important part of what this a game is about in my opinion. I honestly believe it is very similar to putting in golf. If you can go out on the practice green, you put the ball in (the hole) variably more time that not. But it's the pressure the anxiety of the moment and its got nothing to do with your technical and physical skills its got something to do with your mental capacity to block everything else out, and I still believe that is the most underestimated part of what football is about.'
>
> – Sam Newman

Group Round Table Exercise – Implementing Strategies for Honest Feedback

The exercise is called the round-table, and it should be used to build power teams. This practise is extremely powerful when it comes to individual growth. Every week, in a group of between 6 to 10 teammates, one leader at a time will be given feedback from this group only.

This round-table discussion focuses on clearly identifying the #1 strength that this leader brings to the success of the team, and the #1 area for improvement for the success of the team.

After group members have given their feedback, the leader gives feedback on themselves as well. This is a powerful way to elicit growth and team building, and allows members of the group to develop into better people and leaders.

All members of the team from all levels in the organisation should also be asked to join in at some stage to receive a group assessment.

A dramatic amount of growth can take place during these sessions. It is usually incomparably powerful.

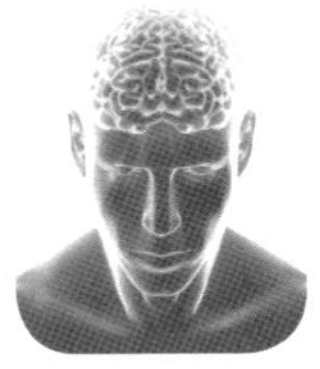

CHAPTER 4

Elite Sports People – Team Success Secrets

The Must-Haves and Must-Not-Haves For Elite Team Success

This is an in-depth and candid series of interviews with some of the world's well-known elite athletes and coaches. We have asked the most pertinent questions when it comes to their experiences creating winning teams, including their essential do's and don'ts.

Their responses opened up enlightening discussions regarding the current state of affairs in both national and international sporting leagues, different styles of leadership and team-building, and, of course, their take on the crucial effect individuals have on their team, from both a positive and a detrimental perspective.

Rechelle Hawkes – Australian Olympic Hockey Team

Clear vision, versatility and a blend of youth is a must

One of Australia's greatest elite athletes, Rechelle Hawkes is one of only two Australian women to win Olympic Gold at three separate Games. Captain of the Australian female hockey team, the Hockeyroos, for eight years, Rechelle has competed in four Olympic Games, winning three Olympic gold medals and a fifth place in Barcelona.

Rechelle is one of the most decorated female hockey players in Australia. During her captaincy tenure of 1993-2000 the Hockeyroos lost only one international tournament.

At the Sydney 2000 Olympic Games, Rechelle was given the rare honour of reading the Olympic Athletes Oath on behalf of all other athletes competing at the Games. Rechelle and the Hockeyroos played a faultless Sydney 2000 Olympic campaign, winning gold and firmly establishing the team as the greatest women's hockey team in the sport's history.

Interview

Must Haves

1. A Blend of Youth and Experience is Essential

"The experienced players should mentor the younger players through the program and ensure that when the more experienced players retire, the younger players are ready to make the step up and assume leadership roles.

"In the 1993 Hockeyroos squad there were very few leaders within the group, so the plan was to build a much bigger foundation of leadership throughout the playing ranks. This included blending the younger generation and the more senior players as often as possible to create a leadership pipeline for years to come.

"The process then was that Ric Charlesworth, the head coach, picked three or four more senior players whom resembled quality on and off-field leadership, 24/7. They were to lead as a united group and include and empower a new group of fresh-faced emerging leaders to step up and take the reins when called upon. This small group expanded over the next two years. In 1995 two co-captains were chosen to lead the team. In 1996, four captains were chosen and the leadership group had increased to 10 players. The entire squad number was 24 players so nearly half the playing group were identified as talented and emerging leaders, so this was nurtured and progressed.

"In 1996, and throughout the many games the team played, the captaincy was shared amongst this larger leadership group. This allowed the players to really support one another and for new leaders to step up and develop their leadership skills under pressure, both on and off the field.

"In 1999, we had no captains whatsoever and it was basically a rotation through the leadership group that had expanded to 12 players. The captaincy was equally shared amongst all leaders within the group. Along the way the vice captaincy positions for each game were allocated to players that were outside of the twelve-strong leadership group. This then allowed these players to develop with the support of the larger leadership group."

2. The Coaches Must Be Versatile and Compliment Each Other

"The Head Coach should bring in coaching support staff that complement him/her and can add value in areas where the Head Coach may have certain weaknesses. The coaching support team should be the best in the business.

"These coaches must know the game inside and out. They must have high analytical skills to dissect the opposition quickly and determine the way forward in the game and under pressure.

"They must be able to bring the team along with them. They need to have command, be respected and drive the team in a direction that they want them to go in. If they don't they will firstly lose the change room, and then the entire team. Half of the respect that you get as a coach is from past experiences and accomplishments; the other half you gain from your actions. This includes how they engage, how they treat individuals, how they set the vision and also how they handle themselves when under pressure.

"The coach needs to pick the right people. They must compliment the team dynamic as a coach and as a player. If they get this wrong it can cause issues that will surmount and hold the team back considerably."

3. A Clear Vision, Strategy and a Common Goal

"Align the mission of the group and ensure all are headed towards a common goal. Leading into Atlanta in 1996 the group signed off on a mission statement and these key aims and value statements guided the team into a successful gold medal campaign.

"The vision must have real sense of purpose, and it must be achievable. There must be a common goal that everyone has bought into and everyone must be ready to roll his or her sleeves up at anytime to get the job done. They have to want to be there and they show this by their actions. When the vision is clear, then there is a movement within the group that can be an unstoppable force. This force brings success and the only way this force can be slowed is by changing the individuals in the group."

4. A Unique and Adaptable Game Plan

"The team game plan/strategy should be unique and different to the opposition and hard to emulate. This gives you the point of difference. A unique strategy, which is well understood by all players, that is executed to the highest level.

"Any great game plan firstly needs simplicity. It must have careful instruction for the team to learn and own it. The group must understand exactly what their role is and the other role of teammates. The quickest way to teach a game plan is by demonstrating and role-playing at training. Evaluating areas of strength and areas in need of improvement will expose chinks in the chain that may need urgent attention. Once there are no chinks in the chain, then the game plan can withstand any amount of pressure when the heat is on.

"Lastly, no team wins without an abundance of talent and an equally matched propensity for hard work. This does not need any further explanation in my opinion."

Must Not Haves

1. A Toxic Culture will Lead to Disappointment

"Toxic culture needs to be curtailed and any offenders who continue to defy team goals and ethos should be removed from the system. Everyone should be on the same page.

"A toxic culture is where you get an individual or a number of individuals who align. They have usually decided that they are not happy with the way the organisation is being run; then there comes a rising up against the coach or certain players within the team. If this issue is allowed to fester and grow legs then it will get out of hand. No team can be successful with a toxic culture. The only way through is to open up the communication vents and encourage further discussion to eliminate and defuse any and all issues. If this is not done as soon as the issues are on the table, then the break down and disharmony will be demonstrated on the field for all to see. Hidden cracks always appear when under pressure.

"If there is a clear vision with rules and guidelines then this sets the benchmark of behaviours and allows for issues to be dealt with effortlessly and easily to ensure the mission goes forth with force. This is usually best done by using an independent person from outside of the organisation to manage."

2. Predictability is a Sure Fire Way to Limit Your Success

"Being adaptable and having the ability to change the way the team plays is essential for continued success. Continuing on with the status quo may mean that good results are achieved initially, however long term and continued success is more difficult to achieve.

"The coach must have the ability to quickly change strategy at anytime. The team must also be willing to adapt to new thinking and do it as one united team on the spot. This takes trust and understanding of the purpose, which then builds an environment that does not complain – complaining is a cancer in any team. To be a high performing team, everyone in the team must be able to have a say and be heard. All team members must know each other's strengths and weaknesses, this allows understanding and flexibility to cover for each other whenever required."

3. Lack of Long-Term Planning.

"This is not having a succession plan in place when players retire, an ability to identify talented young players and mentor them through the system so they can assume leadership roles when senior players retire.

"If you want to maintain sustainable success, and we all know a team has ebbs and flows, it's how long you are going to have that ebb for that really matters. After the Olympic Games players move on; coaches retire or are removed. If the management want to stay at the top of the game and maintain the level of success required then there needs to be a succession plan in place for all coaches and players to transition smoothly in or out. In Ric Chalersworth's case, he was such a brilliant coach, there should have been a succession plan in place as he knew, and we all knew, two years out that he was going to retire after the 2000 Olympics. Looking back, Ric's predecessor should have been anointed 12 months out to Ric's departure. This allows ample time for ease of information sharing, both culturally and strategically.

"I find that there is always a big gap when key management transition in and out of a team. When there was a succession plan in place this gap would be much smaller. This basically means the organisation will be working smarter, not harder, in the pursuit of sustained success."

4. Don't Think it Will Just Happen

"Complacency in sport is one of the biggest issues facing very successful teams.

"We, as leaders, had to ensure that the benchmark was always rising, especially if we had a new young member join the team at any stage. If we didn't then we would get complacent and this would flow onto all our younger team members. When this happens we would not be reaching our best individually and collectively. To do this all players were expected to make sure they were in the best possible condition physically and mentally. We all had to meet the requirements put in place by our dieticians, strength and conditioning coaches, the list goes on. And if we did not reach this agreed benchmark when required then there would be ramifications that would affect the entire team. One in, all in. This created a group focus that required no discussion or elaboration.

"We were worked hard for our gold medals and team success. We knew how to get there and we had great leadership, which fast tracked us all. And we also knew when complacency was creeping in because you can see it and feel it once you have tasted success."

Justin Langer – Australian Cricket Team

Honesty and Hard Work is a Non Negotiable

Justin Langer is a former Australian test cricketer and the current coach of the Western Australian cricket team and the Perth Scorchers. He has played cricket all over the world and has represented Australia in 105 Test matches.

He is most well known for his left-handed batting, which led he and his partner Matthew Hayden to be the most successful Australian opening batsmen in recent years until he retired to go into coaching.

Interview

Must-Haves

1. Work Ethic

"I learned this when I was about 16 years old. My hero was the great Dennis Lillee. He said that there are three secrets of success. The first one is that you've got to work hard. Then he said that the second secret of success is that you've got to work hard! And of course the third secret is to work hard as well! You can imagine a teenager with his head down, embarrassed. I'll never forget that!

"You can tell a good organisation by whether they really work hard in it or not. Ricky Ponting once said that you never meet anyone who gets better at something by doing less of it. And champion individuals and champion teams, in my opinion, work harder than anyone else. There's no secret recipe; there's no magic dust to make champions. They just work harder than everyone else. In corporations. In sports. In the arts. They all work harder! That's number one."

2. Be Honest

"The second most important must-have for winning team success is honesty. You've got to have the courage to speak honestly to people. Because of uncertainty around political correctness, I don't think that people get told the truth enough in the world. Some people don't like this word, because it makes them think of being disciplined by others. People often associate the way I use honesty here with criticising people.

"But at the same time there's a bit of hypocrisy with this approach. Because in most people's minds, it's okay to be honest and tell someone they've done a good job. Or it's okay to pat someone on the back when they're doing well. But if they're not doing well and you tell them the facts, that's being honest as well! You've got to give them honest feedback; at the end of the day it's always been the Australian way to give honest feedback. That's what being honest is about!

"Honesty is more about others pointing out facts, and then you being honest within yourself. If there's honesty within yourself, then it will come out within the team as well, and that's very good. There are very good individuals who are meticulously honest with themselves. You cannot lie to yourself for very long; you can call it your conscience, you can call it whatever you want, but there's something there in everyone! You can bluff everyone else and stay in denial, but you can't lie to yourself.

"I think champions are collectively or individually, meticulously honest with themselves and with other people. And if you're going to be honest with other people you've got to be prepared to take honest feedback as well."

3. Celebrate Successes

"You've got to celebrate success and reward the good days. You have a lot of tough days. In my business you have a lot of bad days. It's better to reward success and better to celebrate success. The thing I miss most about playing test cricket is singing the team song at the end of the test match. You grab a crown lager, put Johnny Williams on, and then belt out the words to the song.

"I was given the privilege – passed down from Ricky Ponting – to be the song master, and that was such a high standing for me and within

Australian cricket culture; so we took it very seriously. It's important to celebrate success, because it helps to build camaraderie. Camaraderie is critical for success, because it's the glue that keeps everything together when you're under pressure. It's like when you're a kid in the schoolyard with your brother, and if he gets in trouble, you're going to stand up for him.

"With someone who you probably don't know that well you just let him go and see what happens. And I would consider that the great Australian cricket team, which I was very lucky to play with, could be my brotherhood. Michael Clark is like my little brother; Steve Waugh is like my big brother. Adam Gilchrist, Glenn McGrath and Matthew Hayden were like my brothers as well; that might sound a bit corny but that's how it was!"

'Camaraderie is critical for success, because it's the glue that keeps everything together when you're under pressure.'

You get a feeling that you would go to war for them any day of the week:

"That camaraderie can be earned by gaining respect on the field and off the field and also celebrating the successes; singing the song or the national anthem. One night I remember that song was sung up in the top storey of a building. All the boys singing the song up there. I remember singing it in the middle of Lords; I remember singing it on the border between Colombo and Kandahar in Sri Lanka. Because that's what we did and they're the most memorable moments."

Justin Langer has written a book called *Australia, You Little* Beauty*. He explains:

"The title is the last line of the Australian team's song; the book is about those moments. Those are the moments that I remember. We were celebrating success, because what are you doing all that hard work for if you're not going to enjoy it? Enjoy the big moments. For me it's a must do and a key to success. You've got to remember the good days."

Langer then speaks about words of wisdom that he heard from Francois Pienaar, a great South African rugby captain:

"He told me once that if you have a good day, you reward yourself. Buy yourself a gift, take yourself out to a nice dinner or something, so you remember the good days and get that feeling of why you are doing this. The reasons you work hard and sacrifice is so you can have the good days. You've got to remember the good days."

4. Develop People As Much As Players

"I think the fourth thing, which is a critical must-do is that you've got to develop people as much as players. There's so much talent around! While there are lots of people with talent, you still know the guys who are going to be successful under pressure and make the right choices on and off the cricket field. Characters with good integrity.

"This is why you've got to develop good people as well as good athletes. Because if you just develop them as footy players, cricket players, and even stock brokers in a broader context, that's not that reliable. You might succeed; you might not. However, those results can be quite fickle.

"Instead, a safer alternative is to develop good people. If you get a good culture and great people, and you improve individual behaviour, you end up with great people who make good decisions and have good behaviours and a good culture. You've got to develop the people as much as the players."

Must-Not-Haves

1. You Must Not Neglect the Little Things

"You must keep an eye on the little things! Nigel Ray, who owns the Saracens Rugby Union Football team in London, is one of the most successful people and one of the greatest mentors in London. He once told me that when you start a business, you count the paper clips. You count everything! You know exactly what is what.

"In a lot of businesses, the owners get successful and start neglecting the little things. They forget about the little expenses and the belt buckle gets a bit sloppy. They forget and neglect the little things at their own peril; neglect the little disciplines at their own peril – on and off the field; in and out of the office. If you've got the little things right, the big things look a lot easier."

In both sports and a wider context this is often related to disappointment as well, but Langer insists that this is not the case:

"The pain of discipline is nothing like the pain of disappointment. Discipline doesn't mean sitting under freezing cold ice baths and meditating; discipline is about making good choices about everything all the time. To me that's what discipline is about.

"Neglect those little disciplines at your own peril.

"If you make bad choices, you might think they are little at first, but they have a tendency to snowball and they end up being big later on. If you can't do the little things, well it's going to be difficult when you walk out in front of 100,000 people in the MCG! It's going to be hard to make good choices when you're under pressure. The first must-not is that you must not neglect the little things."

2. You Must Not Get Complacent

"This goes hand-in-hand with the first one – complacency is like poison. You've got to be careful about complacency and the only time the Australian cricket team lost … I still remember it. In 2005 we lost the Ashes. We won everything else, but we lost the Ashes! That was the only time we got a bit complacent.

"Complacency is like poison.

"John Buchanan, who's a brilliant coach with a brilliant vision, let us go a bit for about 12 months. I went with the approach too; that is, *no, they know how to handle things now and we're just going to let them go."*

While it's human nature to fall back and become complacent instead of speaking up and initiating change, Langer talks about the part he played in the complacence and his awakening from it:

"I still remember two things, and this might sound really strange! When we played New Zealand before the 2005 Ashes had been lost, I remember reading a book called *Shantaram*. It's about a one thousand-page book and right from the two days before the last test, to the day of the last test, I read the whole book!

"What am I talking about? Well, there was nothing wrong with the book itself, but what I realised was that I was so relaxed about how we were going that I was reading a book! This insight left me thinking that's not me! I had to admit that wasn't at all me; I was supposed to be in the game. When you're in the game you're in the game. You're not on vacation. You're supposed to be like prize fighters!"

Langer speaks about how he was relaxed and complacent:

"But no, I was so relaxed, I read all of *Shantaram*. Every night, Hayden and I would have a glass of wine and a cheese platter after dinner. I swear, we were like prize fighters – ripped – yet every night just relaxed, and still winning everything."

The festivities didn't last too long:

"But it came back to bite us in the rear, and we had to let go of that complacence. If under pressure you get just a bit complacent, you're in danger. That's when England put us under more pressure than we expected they would, and we still won the first test. We won in three days.

"Instead of waking us up, it made us go even more complacent. Another Ashes and we're in this party mode. Not all of our guys may admit it, but that's how I felt. We're the Australian cricket team and we get complacent and get bitten in the backside.

"It happens often in business and it happens in sporting teams as well. Don't get complacent!"

3. You Must Not Accept Mediocrity

"Don't accept mediocrity. This doesn't mean that you have to take a sledgehammer approach, because by this time it's often too late and mediocrity is engrained in the culture. Some coaches are always neglecting the little things that lead to general mediocrity and then think they can fix the problem by dropping four guys from their test team. Sledgehammer approach."

Being a coach is about challenge and it's not challenging to scapegoat people and apply a band-aid to a deeper problem:

"That's not tough to me, that's the easy way out. What's tough is telling someone who is being mediocre every single day of their life. You have to ask them what they are doing and how it's working for them. That takes courage! Leadership isn't a popularity contest; you're going to get people angry with you. It's very, very hard to look someone in the eye everyday and tell them they need to try harder.

"But if you don't want to accept the mediocrity, then that's what you have to do. You can't accept mediocrity and poor behaviours. One of the worst sayings in Australian culture is, "She'll be alright, mate." This is ridiculous. What will be alright? Will it be alright by itself if you don't do anything about it?"

Mediocrity gets you nowhere. Champions have visions and they go out and make them a reality:

"You must not accept mediocrity! You can't accept it. Mediocrity gets you nowhere. Champions have got big visions and they're hungry for more. And if you're hungry, you're not mediocre. The champions haven't got a single mediocre bone in their body. You must not accept mediocrity in anything you do. On the field and off the field."

4. Never Lose Sight of Your Vision

Everyday pressures can get athletes to forget their vision, and this is one thing that can unravel winning team success:

"You must not ever lose sight of your vision or the bigger picture. One thing I've learned as a coach is that when you're a player you've got your own personal vision. You could be the best player in the world, but when you become a coach, everything is about the bigger picture. You always look at the bigger picture and I think you must not ever lose sight of your vision or your dream."

Justin Langer says that this element is important as it gives you the energy and inspiration that you need on a daily basis:

"Your vision keeps you moving forward. If you lose sight of it in a team – or, in a wider context, in your company or even in your family – you may start accepting mediocrity and you may start saying things will be okay instead of doing something about them.

"If you've got a vision, and you know exactly what it is and you can hold your nerve, that will give you your energy and inspiration. So you must not lose sight of your vision. You've got to put all your day-to-day attention toward being great at the little things. And that's always a balancing act.

"Your vision keeps you moving forward."

It's not just important to have a vision, it's also important to develop a methodology to achieve it:

"If you have your vision, you also have to give your attention to the processes and outcome. If you want to score 100 runs, or if you want to be the best player, you can only do that by giving 100% attention to every aspect of the task; that's called concentration.

"Essentially, don't lose sight of the bigger picture or the vision; you do that and I reckon you're dead in the water."

Ben Graham – AFL & NFL Captain

Do Your Job, Drop the Ego, and Be Ready

A former Australian Rules Football player who moved to the United States and became a punter for the New York Jets of the National Football League. He also played for a range of teams in the NFL such as the New Orleans Saints, Arizona Cardinals and the Detroit Lions.

When Graham played for the Geelong Football Club, between 1993 and 2004, he played 219 games. He has not played for any other AFL team. He is most often noted for his ability to kick extremely long and accurate distances. He is the only player in the world to become a captain in the AFL and the NFL. He played in the AFL Grand Final in 1995 and also the Super Bowl XLIII in 2009.

Interview

He compared his experience in playing football in the two regions and also his experience coaching following retirement.

Must-Haves

When asked about the things that a team must have, Ben Graham's response was focused on his experiences in the NFL in the United States. He compared Australian football culture in many of his responses and examples. The first must-haves he spoke about were:

1. Do Your Job and Let Others Do Theirs

"The number one value at the four NFL clubs that I played with was *do your job and trust the guy next to you to do his*. So everything was about only controlling what you can control and that is the one skill you bring to the team."

Graham spoke of his specific experience as a punter.

"So I had to keep my spot on the team and, to give my team the best chance of winning, I had to do my job and trust that the guys around me are going to do theirs. So in my position as punter I was to trust that the long snapper would get the ball to me, where it's supposed to be. I had to trust that the guys at the line would protect the punt and not have it blocked. Then I had to trust that those down the field would get the tackle so that we gave the other team poor field position.

"So the must-do in that is that it doesn't really matter who you're playing for, whether you're playing in a Super Bowl or a regular season game, it's all about doing your job and trusting the guy next to you is going to do his."

Ben Graham speaks of a common question he gets in interviews:

"I'll never forget leading into the Super Bowl in 2009, there's that big question: whether you should treat it like the biggest game in the world or just another game. And I treated it just like another game. Nothing changes; you still have to do your job. Don't worry about anything else."

The second most important thing in team success, from his experience based in American football and sporting culture, is a focus on talent:

2. Pure Talent

"They recruit on talent, they perform on talent, success comes with talent and you can't live without it. The best systems might be able to gloss over the fact that they might not have the most talented list, but at the end of the day you need a talented quarterback, you need a talented running back and a talented wide receiver.

"A lot of the decisions recruiters make when it comes to the NFL, given that most of the talent comes out of their college system, is that they pick the most talented players over any character issues they may have. Once you're playing in the NFL, there is no development or welfare program to continue to develop players in that area. When they come out of college they've got their education, they've proven to be great college footballers, and so it's purely based around talent."

Commenting on whether the recruiter is the most important person in the make up who picks the talent, Graham responded:

"The pro personnel they have – the scouting they have in America – is unbelievably expansive. They're right across the country. They have recruiters in every network and school: all of the 117 Division 1 colleges; hundreds of Division 2 colleges."

As a result, not many players get missed:

"I would say that they are the most important person, because of the way the cut-throat nature of the industry is. If a player gets recruited and he's no good, he will get released and it won't cost the club any money. In Australia a list manager has to find the talent, develop the talent and then deliver on their promises. They know they'll play at the club for 3, 4, 5, 10 years; their job is just to bring the talent and then, with that talent, the coach's responsibility is to put the strategy together and play it for success."

Graham specifies that character in life is secondary in the American football culture:

"I've had close up experiences with teammates where they have been high draft picks, high talent, a lot of money has been invested in them, but yet they're some of the worst individuals you'll ever meet. They are poor teammates. They have a poor character. They break the law. They have no respect for authority. Yet because they've got high talent they continue to play. Now whether that's right or wrong, it just goes to show that character comes second to talent over there."

Then Ben Graham spoke about another must-have in the American perspective. If things are to go smoothly, everyone must have a short-term view of different situations:

3. A Short-Term View

"The third ingredient to success over there is a short-term view; a short-term look at the game; a short-term look at recruiting. Short-term. Things turn over so quickly in the NFL that if you don't have a short-term view, a *win now* philosophy, it's seen as though you'll never get anywhere; you'll never become successful. The teams with a longer-term view, with too many project players, they don't develop as quickly as you would like.

"Essentially, it's a *win now* philosophy. So, for example, when I got cut from the New Orleans Saints and I had a workout at the Arizona Cardinals, they cut me a punter, because they were looking for someone, they wanted an upgrade in that position. They wanted a short-term solution for a play-off run."

This happened in week 13 of the regular season, with only four weeks left to go:

"They were making changes mid-season to ensure that they gave themselves the best opportunity to win when it came to play-offs, and I was part of that, given my ability to pin opposition teams with the drop punt. So they cut Dirk Johnson and signed me and eight weeks later I was playing in the Super Bowl.

"It's a *win now* philosophy, it's not about right or wrong, because the system is based on a year-by-year proposition in the NFL. Only the very, very good clubs and the very well ranked clubs that have high talent on their lists can sustain success for a long period of time. I'll give you an example. I had a teammate called Ryan Myers who busted his ass every week through three training camps. He knew his stuff inside and out. He wasn't the highest talented kid, and now the Jets pro personnel ranked him the 257th ranked line backer in the country. When Cody Spencer was released from Tennessee Titans, he was ranked 210th on their line backer chart. They cut Ryan, they signed Cody and that very next week Cody turned the wrong way on a punt protection and I had my first NFL punt block. They wanted an upgrade in that position in week three in the NFL season just because they thought someone was hiring talent. It doesn't always pay off, but it's in general a short-term philosophy to get instant success. This is what drives NFL clubs."

4. A Lack of Loyalty and A Lot of Money

"In the American system, there is next-to-zero loyalty for clubs in the NFL. Players hang their hats on their college careers. They love their college experience; they love their college team. It's almost just a matter of fact that they play NFL.

"The team they play for is really inconsequential to a lot of them, because it's a job. They wouldn't be playing it if they weren't getting paid like they do in the AFL. There's no local talent. Three percent of high school footballers go on to play college football; three percent of college footballers go on to play in the codes. And the guys who don't make it don't play anywhere else.

"The fact is it's a job; it's well rewarded if you're good at it."

In some cases, some players have the ability to afford things that the NFL clubs don't offer. Services such as coaching in leadership, public speaking, personal trainers, and fitness trainers, are a few examples:

"Players go to great lengths to make sure that they get the very best out of themselves because they know that they have a short-term opportunity to earn what could be a lot of money."

This allows for young players coming up through the ranks without a lot of money to back themselves on talent and then later on outsource themselves to that support level:

"The NFL clubs don't have any program to d
no developmental academy. And that reall
I learned to kick well was by repetition: 10
good coach and I went to a punting camp.

"The Jets did send me there, but my special teams coach had no idea about the specific techniques of punting. In our first meeting he asked me what concerns me most about coming from another country to play sport. And I said, 'My age. I feel like I'm too old in your eyes.' He said he couldn't care less if I was fifty. He said, 'If you can kick the ball down the field with good hang time, you'll play until you're fifty.'

"For them it's all about the talent. If you've got the talent, they don't want to nurture it and develop it; they don't have the time for it. I got cut three times in one year, because they thought that there was more talent out there. They didn't want to spend the time on developing me – they preferred to sign someone else.

"That happens right across the league in every position. So there's no development! There is minimal welfare. When I first got to America my wife was blown away because we half expected to be given some advice and some assistance when we were trying to find a house, car, schools for the kids. Even with all the little things that need to be set up for an Australian in America, they had one person that was almost too busy to help – a past player who wanted to be a coach: just a token effort. And it shows how the NFL Players Association are going through a rigorous change to their program right now, because it identified that 78% of NFL players, three years after they finish playing, are broke, are divorced, can't afford their medical bills, are depressed, are on drugs, and, in the most tragic cases, some commit suicide. It's a horrific number. There's not enough support ile players are playing to make that transition to life after football. So they're making an effort now. But after I was an assistant for eight years, I'd seen so many kids come from nothing, get the world at their feet, and then – for one reason or another – struggle ever since."

Ben Graham agreed to the description of the situation as a massive human scrapheap:

"There are no lower levels; there's nowhere else to go. And that's where the players that are able to make a successful NFL career come in with a very serious focus to make the absolute most of it. They understand that the club can't give them certain things, so they're going to get as fit as they can, get as strong as they can. I worked with the wide receiver and quarterback in the off-season so I could learn my craft as quickly as I could. So once I got to training camp I was ready. I didn't leave a single stone unturned. It didn't matter how far or wide I'd gone to get it, I was going to make this team."

Must-Not-Haves

Ben Graham then spoke about the things that you mustn't do as a player, a coach or as an organisation to jeopardise your chances of being a winning team. Again, his responses are based on comparing his experiences in the United States to Australia:

1. Do Not Think You Are Bigger Than The Team

"From a player's perspective we just talked about doing your job, having talent, and individually outsourcing professional help. It's very much of an individual flavour. The biggest, must-not-do is to think that you as an individual are bigger than the team.

"A common saying in the States is that a game is won or lost during the week. So if you've done everything to plan, the coaches have planned, you've strategised what you need to do as a team to beat the opposition. If you get to the weekend and you think you know more than that, or you've asked to run a specific route and you think you know better and go and do something on your own – run a different route, or do something the coaches haven't asked to do – that's the biggest must-not. Because you need to make sure that every single player on the field, on a Sunday, plays their role.

"It can be compared to a well-oiled machine, like the New England Patriots have proven to be. This is key ingredient to success. You must not think that you are bigger than the team."

2. Do Not Treat Football Like A Hobby

"The number two must-not in the United States is to do as AFL players do sometimes and treat the sport like a hobby. They treat it like it's something that they've already done. Another common saying in the NFL is to *treat it like it's a privilege, not a right*. So therefore it's a job.

"They have to treat it like a job because if they don't, if they think it's a fun thing to do to pass the time – what a cool, fun thing to tell their kids, that you played in the NFL – then time passes them by really quickly.

"When players start drifting away from the job aspect, it gets compared to companies like Apple and IBM, bigger corporate companies, where people turn up to work on time, every time. Five minutes early is five minutes late, everything is like clockwork.

"One thing I loved about the NFL is how scheduled everything was. Everything was always in place. The guys that took the piss or treated it like it was a bit of fun, or turned up late, didn't last very long at all. They get their mobile phone going off in the middle of a meeting, or someone falling asleep in a meeting and the whole premise behind it is that if you don't do your job they'll turf you and get someone else who will."

From a coaching perspective and from a player perspective they treat it like a job. Ben Graham suggests that Australian footballers do treat the sport as if it's fun and not as if it's a job:

"Given the culture, and given that you can play locally, and given that there are probably some AFL players who would still be playing football if they weren't getting paid any money, it therefore gives them an out to not treat it like a job. They still see it as a bit of fun and a hobby and don't take it quite as seriously as they should.

The level of professionalism in the AFL can definitely step up a notch. And it will gradually, and it has since I've been playing, but it could still improve."

3. Leave Nothing to Chance

In the NFL, the modus operandi was to leave nothing to chance. Teams, players, coaches and in general everyone was expected to be prepared for anything:

"There's no luck in it over there. What stood out to me from my time before that in the AFL was that in Australia they were even reluctant to have too many meetings. It's almost as if they are reluctant to look after their players. On game day the coaches almost just step back and allow the players to do what they want. There's a lot of luck involved in a lot of aspects of football in Australia. There's even luck in how the ball bounces.

"In the NFL the game is won or lost during the week with how the players prepare and how the coaches prepare for the players. They talk about how if you don't know your role, then you cannot play fast enough. They are expected to play fast, so they must know what it takes to play their role.

"So by that, the hours spent learning about your role didn't put it into perspective. During training camp at the start of the year a new player might get a play-book with a thousand plays in it. And every week they'll pull out 200 plays for the opposition. You'll know those plays back to front and inside and out. They've even got it as specific as if they run a play during practice that didn't come up, they wouldn't use it in the game because they didn't trust it would work.

"Everything that was done during the week sets up the weekend and leaves nothing to chance on the weekend. And as a player, as a punter, I knew that there were so many things I had to do with my technique to get me ready for Sunday. I couldn't just turn up on Sunday and think that because I could kick a football I could roll out of bed and punt the ball sixty yards down the field.

"There was no guesswork – the minute you started thinking whether this is a good punt or not you were screwed. Because with everything that was going on with the pressures of playing an NFL game, you had to make sure that you had done exactly what you needed to do, which left nothing to chance so you could be as successful as you could be."

4. Not Playing Your Role

"The last must-not-do is to not play your role. It's the flip side of what I spoke about earlier. If the New England Patriots are a well-oiled machine, it's because of the systems that are put into place by the coaches that allow players to do what they need to do."

So if someone gets hurt, or if someone gets cut, other players come in and take over:

"You can't allow anything to be player driven. Players in the NFL, if they were given a chance to have decision making capacities at any level, it would be a recipe for disaster. The systems that are put in place by the management and the coaches are what makes the team successful. All they need to do is make sure the players tie in, but not give them any opportunity to dictate, because they all have their own individual agendas to be the very best they can be. So in the successful organisations the players buy into the structures and the systems and the strategies that are put forward, and if they put their head down and work as hard as they can then they want to learn their play-book, and put all the strategies into place that enable them to play fast and to play their role. So when you talk about the must-nots, the organisations that aren't successful give the players – especially their high profile, highly paid players – more responsibility to run the show."

Ben Graham's experience in the NFL shows us just how seriously success can be chased. As in all areas, there are team members who have their own agendas; the true method to achieving success is by developing a trust within your team – everyone working to the best of their abilities to achieve the same goal. The keen focus of an NFL player, with such a short window to carve out a career, is something we should all admire and hope to replicate.

Al Westover – NBL Championship Coach

Motivated, Mentally Tough Team Players

Al Westover is a premium professional basketball coach with a successful career that spans a total of seven nations. Westover played professional basketball for the Melbourne Tigers in the National Basketball League (NBL) before going onto success at seven Victorian Basketball League (VBA) championships and one South Eastern Australian Basketball League (SEABL) championship.

Westover was also assistant coach to Lindsay Gaze for 14 years at the Melbourne Tigers, during which time the team won a gold medal, won two grand finals, and was runner up in two others. Westover coached the Melbourne Tigers to the 2006 and 2008 NBL championships. He has been an All-Star coach and coached two seasons in Japan's premier Basketball Japan League (BJ). The Shiga Lakestars have had their best seasons in the team's history since Westover has been with them.

Must-Haves

1. A Talented Team

Al Westover began by explaining his first must-have for a winning team:

"First of all you have to have talented players that are team guys; whom put the team first.

"You need a certain level of talent to win championships – either in skills or in knowledge. Talent is physical ability, as well as players that have smarts and play smart. Fellows that put the team first.

"I've always told our guys every year I coach that it's an easy game to play as long as you don't care who gets the credit."

He further clarified:

"It also needs a bit of unity – a common goal. It needs talented team players whom have a team goal. I've seen a lot of talented players in basketball that will have great stats, but won't be winning players. They need to put their team first and be willing to make individual sacrifices for the greater good."

2. A Motivated Group

Westover continued by explaining the second must-have for a winning team:

"For the next one, it's with your group. You need a group that's very motivated and coaches can help with that; obviously it's part of our job.

"Any player that's going to be good is going to be self-motivated.

Any team that is good is going to be very self-motivated from within. And if I always have to motivate, and the players don't have that motivation themselves, eventually that falls on deaf ears.

"That motivation could come from within, or it could come from leadership."

3. Mental Toughness

The third must-have for a winning team is mental toughness:

"All these areas overlap with each other, with mental toughness. This goes with any sport at any level. Look at the teams in the NBL or the NFL. Probably everyone is the same size or the same weight. They have similar characteristics speed wise and all that.

"So really the game is played more with the mind, than the body. To be mentally tough, that covers so many things: you've got to bring your commitment every day. You can't pick and choose.

"Like Jerry West said, you can't just work on the days you feel good, you might not feel right, you might be a little banged up, but you've got to bring it every day. Because that pushes your teammates and makes you better."

Admitting that this is hard at times:

"Sometimes that's easier said than done, when the weather gets cold or whatever. If you're on the road you can get distracted by the crowds. It takes players who are mentally tough.

"You go through good patches and bad patches, if you have a bad patch you can't drop your head, you have to stay positive and aggressive. That takes someone who's mentally tough.

"You're going to have bad calls, by referees and umpires. And it's part of the game, and I know it infuriates everyone, but you can't linger on that, you've got to get over it. You've got to think about the next play. A lot of that is learning to play in the moment."

4. An Ability to Make Adjustments

Championship players and championship teams also need a critical component:

"They have to have the ability to make adjustments."

How adaptability works in sports and scouting:

"In any team in any sport nowadays, everyone does lots of scouting and all. So you've got to make adjustments to your play. When we have our offence we might run a cut long line and the defence might not have the fore sense to do that and they might take that away; now we have to make an adjustment and do a different type of cut or a different type of screenings.

"That's why coaches do all the video work and breakdown stuff and all that. You've got to see how the opposition is playing you and how you can punish what they're doing.

"Consequently you can see how the other team is doing and take their best player out. So depending on your personnel and the other team's personnel, if you're a player who's bad with your right hand, your opposing team's going to figure it out. You can go right into their offence, or make the adjustment and go the other way. I think that's the key: you have to make adjustments.

"Sometimes it has to be at half time. You have to make adjustments on the spot and that's very important."

Must-Not-Haves

1. 'The Disease of Me'

Getting right to the heart of the matter, Westover states the biggest must-not-have for a winning team:

"The first thing that could unravel a team, and I've seen a lot of it in basketball and football, both big team sports and small team sports. Pat Reilly calls it 'the disease of me'."

Patrick James Riley, currently an American professional basketball executive, is president of Miami Heat in the NBA. He is esteemed as one of the greatest basketball coaches of all time and has also written a book, *The Disease of More*, which goes in-depth on these issues.

Commenting on success, Westover says:

"If you have success sometimes players say, 'I want to play more and I want to score more'.

"Your goals should always be good, but you have to help the team.

'So *the disease of me* is a player getting more concerned about themselves than the team. It probably happens in football, but in basketball you have all the stats, and who scored what."

This issue can get out of control and manifest in different ways as well:

"One year, a bad year, it wasn't just a disease of me but a disease of 'my buddy'. More playing time for your 'friend'. When you guys are teammates it should be equal respect across the board.

"Maybe you don't have to like each other and maybe you don't have to be best friends, but you definitely have to respect each other. What happened in our bad year was a bit of a disease of me and 'my buddy' and the group became quite cliquey. A couple of little groups.

"Once that happens they descend into little groups and it's cliquey; you know what's going to come out of that. No good is going to come of that.

"It is very difficult to fix this once it's already set in hard."

2. A Lack of Enthusiasm

On the other end of the spectrum of motivation, a lack of enthusiasm can really kill a team:

"You may not have good enthusiasm, you may not have good team spirit, you may not have good leaders. Like I say, a coach has to motivate and inspire, but this has to come from the group too.

"So you've got players who are getting on with each other. 'Come on! You're not running back!'

"They're pushing each other, demanding that from themselves, stepping up. Teams that don't have good leadership, they kind of wallow, and they're going to suffer.

"One year I had new players in, two young guards from America, and we were starting over again and I thought talent wise that group could compete for a championship. But they didn't handle the pressure of expectation well, from the club and from maybe the media.

"We saw the pressure at games from the opposition and I thought a lot of the reason why we didn't have the pressure was – and we could say it was a new group, a lot of new players, but the bottom line was – we didn't have leadership within the group.

"You need a group that is strong, mentally tough and has leadership. When we didn't have players stepping up and saying, 'That was my bad, my mistake', they started blaming others instead.

"Players, coaches; we've all got to accept the blame. Accept it, be a man about it. Teams that do that usually get better and improve; teams that start pointing fingers and blaming others, that's a spiral to utter failure. Nothing more sure than that!"

3. A Lack of Adaptability

Lack of enthusiasm is tied in with a lack of adaptability:

"I guess you could also say that teams that fail don't make adjustments. I think you see it in any sport, especially early in the season. There might be a few surprises; they might get a few wins. Maybe it's surprising that they win the first two or three and they're not expecting to do well.

"Then what happens – you see it a lot of times in the NBL – new players come in. Maybe they do well at first, and then teams are scouting and figuring them out. And they are not able to make adjustments.

"They might force the issue, anxiety levels might go up, which creates frustration and disharmony within the group. The good teams and the good players will make those adjustments and keep finding ways to win. But mediocre players and mediocre teams, once they're figured out, aren't able to make the adjustments and win. And that's a big thing I think in sport."

4. A Lack of Flow and Team Unity

Commenting on the importance of having the management, board and players all flowing in the right direction, Westover says:

"Without it there wouldn't be much success, and challenges as a coach become more difficult

"When I first took over the Tigers we all seemed to work really well together, then later on it seemed like the owners were off doing their own thing – they weren't connecting with the players and the coaching staff as much. It's not just about the owner; it's not just about the coach; and not just the players. All three need to be working together and connected.

"And if something is lacking then there are breakdowns; and those things can spiral and get worse.

"One year we were in four straight finals, then we pulled out of the league and we came back and then some players had to take massive pay cuts, while some didn't.

"And that created a chasm right there between ownership and the players. Players always like to feel the management is behind them 100%. I was telling them that they could play for half the money – take it or leave it.

"All of a sudden your players' allegiance and their loyalty levels taper off.

"Maybe you don't play with the same enthusiasm, passion or leadership. That becomes contagious and leads to cliquey groups and all that.

"So I thought a lot of problems we had came from that. I wasn't going to say that publicly at the time, but that was a problem with the ownership at the time."

The management talk a bit, but it was butting heads against the wall in the end:

"It was tough times; you can go through tough times in basketball, but you find the coaches and the players that are pretty resilient."

Frank Ponissi – NRL Premiership Football Manager

Guardian of the Values of the Culture

Frank heads up the Football Operations at the Melbourne Storm in the NRL. In 2012 the Storm were premiership winners. Frank has also been a specialist coach at a range of rugby teams on the global stage, including South Africa, UK, France and Australia. Frank Ponissi played the game between 1982 and 1992.

Between 1995–1997 he was involved with three consecutive ARL Grand Finals with Manly-Warringah, including the 1996 Premiership.

Interview

Must-Haves

1. Take Pressure Off the Head Coach

"Well my number one is to take as much pressure off the head coach as you can. His role normally is to coach the football team and the players. The more obstacles and interference he has, the more it's going to make his job harder.

"Whether it's discipline issues, retention, recruitment, communication with staff, long-term planning – I'll take control of that. It's absolutely vital that he's inclusive of all those decisions (discipline, long-term planning, recruitment, retention) but I don't want to burden him with long meetings that are drawn out."

Essentially you have to be like a filter:

"At the end of the day, I'll do it so that just gives him the time to worry about how this weekend's going."

2. Guard the Values of the Culture

The second must-have for winning team success is to be a guardian of the values in culture:

"I see myself as a guardian of the values in our culture. It's obvious that these values are driven by the head coach, the senior players and then all the other players, but especially the senior players, and our leadership group.

"Certainly within the group the players are continually responsible for driving each other. Just to get that, we maintain that everyone does their job. And so probably the key word, to finish there, is in accountability. That everyone's accountable."

3. Trust and Delegate

He speaks about his role as a leader. Mainly to trust and delegate:

"That's my role anyway. If you give someone a job you've got to trust them. You've got to trust and delegate; don't become a power control freak.

"And then let them do their job. Keep an eye on them and make sure they're doing their job properly; you don't want to be interfering with people, and double-guessing people and doubting people and questioning people, because that just erodes confidence in them. Basically, if you're very specific in telling people what their job is, what they can and can't do, then let them get on with it. You only have to interfere if the job's not being done properly."

4. Just Enjoy the Game!

Winning teams must also learn to enjoy the game and not take it too far:

"This gets right to the heart of the modern day game: you've just got to enjoy it! You know, at the end of the day, we all started in this game, as kids, because we enjoyed doing it. Now we occasionally still have a beer in the dressing room after the game. We don't get stupid and there are protocols, but it's okay to have a beer after the game. As the staff – and after the play is finished – then why not do this together and enjoy each other's company?"

5. Camaraderie

One of the key aspects of a winning culture is to not bring shame or bad reputation to the team:

"We're big on making sure our players say please, thank you and so on to hotel staff, airport staff, and just use their manners in general. Our policy is about not ever being arrogant or rude to people.

"In essence, it's treating people like adults; if you treat them like school kids, they'll behave like school kids."

Must-Not-Haves

1. Tell No Lies

Honesty is one of the most important parts of a winning team culture. You cannot tell any lies if you are to be successful:

"You can't hide the truth; you've got to be absolutely up-front. Sometimes, you can't avoid holding the truth back or delivering it in a brutal way, but don't tell lies! Don't make up things; players don't like it; staff don't like it. At the end of the day honesty is the best way, but sometimes even honesty is that you've got to remember you're dealing with adults. So, again, if you're telling someone the truth that they're not wanted for next year, player or staff, you do it in a manner that they're still not going to like, but at least they'll respect you for that, rather than being too direct, or too brutal. I think that's a big one."

2. Cut the Corridor Talk

It's also important to be up front in a winning team culture. Although Frank Ponissi agrees that it's human nature that people talk and gossip at times, you have to talk about things out in the open in practice. This is simply the only way to team unity:

"If you've got something to say be upfront about it!

"Once you begin discussing things behind closed doors – once the corridor whispers start – it's not great for the organisation. Sometimes someone will say, 'Personally, I don't agree with the way that we're doing that, but I commit to the cause of what's best for the team.' This is one of our mantras. If you've got something to say be upfront about it! Even if you don't agree, just commit!"

3. Don't Over Do It

When do coaches take breaks? Ponissi addresses a significant part of the coaching scene, where players and other staff are expected to be available at all hours:

"It's easy to let it out, to let it all overtake your life. Your phone could go 24/7 and you just can't allow that. What I'm saying is you've got to be available.

"However, you've also just got to let yourself be able to switch off as well at times. It's easier said than done. If you don't switch off at certain times it can have an effect on your personal life and also has an effect on your longevity in the job because it's a very, very demanding industry.

"When you get a break, take a break. That's how you do it so that it doesn't engulf your life. You have to. You're sitting there at home ... I try to walk in the door and I just can't let something bad out of my mind – it's very hard. If there's an urgent call, earlier on I used to take it at home. But if you get home and you're on the phone for another hour, then you might as well have stayed in the office. So now I screen the calls; if it's urgent I talk to them."

4. Don't Let Your Moods Dictate

Frank Ponissi then talks briefly about the importance of mood management:

"It's very important that you must always manage your moods and body language at all times, because your mood's really important; more so than I ever thought. My body language is important. I learnt that in our critical year in 2010, that salary kept me in; people were generally worried because of the body language.

"It has a role on the effect of the players and the staff, so, again, you can't do it all the time. If you do, all these things build up and it affects your body language and your moods. It has a role on your staff and your players; it's a massive one."

Chris Nunn – AIS Paralympic High Performance Coach

Selling the Vision with Purpose is All You Need!

Chris Nunn was trained as a physical educator with coaching qualifications, and quickly became the first full-time coach – in the world – employed to coach athletes with disabilities. Nunn has been a key player in the Australian Institute of Sport in the 1990s: he opened and operated Canberra's biggest swim school in 2006, and has also worked as a manager at the Australian Paralympic Committee.

Chris Nunn has also attended 7 Paralympic Games between 1988 and 2014. He was Chef de Mission at the Sochii Games in 2014. He received the Order of Australia Medal in 2002, the Dawn Fraser Coach Award in 2000, Paralympic Coach of the Year Award in 1998 and the Rotary International Paul Harris Fellowship.

Interview

Must-Haves

1. A Clearly Defined Vision of the Future

"You've got to have a very clear, defined vision of where you want to take the program. No matter what it is you are dealing with, you need to know where you want to go. It's out of this vision that all the things you will need to do to achieve will become clear."

Once you have defined your vision, it becomes the benchmark for all of your decisions:

"The vision becomes a referral point when you're talking about which direction to take. If you haven't got that clear vision, then it's really hard for people to get on board and understand where you're heading. By defining the vision everyone in the organisation, from the accountant to the janitorial staff, can understand how their role contributes to where the team is going. If you don't do this, you won't get by.

"Be as clear as possible with your vision."

2. Selling the Vision

You must sell your vision at every different level and with every point of contact you have:

"Sell the vision to everyone who will engage with your team. They have to understand it. It is a matter of them knowing what their role is; you've got to sell it to potential sponsors and supporters; you've got to sell your vision to everybody.

"There's got to be no misunderstanding about where you're taking the program or the team. It's what you're trying to achieve.

"Let people understand what you're doing and what you're on about. If they understand you, they understand what the team is going to need. You've got to be the salesperson to make your team work."

Taking an inclusive approach to your sales pitch is critical:

"Part of selling is taking an inclusive attitude when it comes to your sales pitch. In other words, I'm happy to talk to anyone I meet about it, because at some stage I might make contact with someone who has something to offer once they realise where the team is heading. You go as high as you want; even governments and corporations are interested. There are many opportunities for athletes, players and teams; you just need to sell your vision to those people who in some way may be able to assist."

3. Define Everyone's Roles and How That Contributes to the Vision

The third must-have for winning team success, according to Chris Nunn, is to define everyone's roles within the vision:

"Understanding your role and what you're responsible for doing, from leadership all the way down, is the first step. Once you've done that, appreciate that every one of us is different and we are not looking to make clones of our leaders; we want to identify that there are individuals who will come into the team and make a significant contribution. We appreciate it; we accept it and we value it.

"Incoming athletes, coaches and staff must understand their role, the responsibility and the value that they bring to the team in achieving the collective mission and vision. This is what's important. Without understanding roles and responsibilities, lines get crossed and confusion occurs. It really becomes an established protocol that if you want something done then you go to the person who is responsible for doing it."

Everyone in the organisation is important and needs to be on board with the vision:

"Even the janitorial staff play a role in getting things done efficiently for the coach and athlete. I encouraged the athletes living in the Australian Institute of Sport to get to know the janitorial staff by name. They would see them each morning, and by encouraging good manners and a personable approach to others, the athletes got to know these staff. The importance of this relationship was realised if a room was locked, because the cleaners had keys to everything! So as a result of developing a good relationship, if a room was locked and someone couldn't get in, the cleaners were happy to assist."

4. Support Everyone in Their Role

"The most critical thing in achieving your vision, from a leadership perspective, is to support everybody in their role. Provide support when it is required so that they can do their job. From an athlete's perspective, it's all of the sports sciences, physiotherapy, psychology, performance analysis, video analysis, data collection, and so on that they need."

From the point of view of the management staff, it's more about making sure that they have all the information they need to make decisions. Nunn details some of the examples to focus on:

"Make decisions about the long-term plan, the long-term goals, the long-term budget, the breakdown: all of the information that's required for people to get their jobs done better. The process needs to be open, transparent and undertaken in a supportive role. So really, true leadership comes from being able to support people doing their jobs.

"Support comes from recognition of leadership; supporting somebody who's taking initiative, such as an athlete, who does the right thing. That's the support that comes from good leadership, and providing it is imperative. Without support the team unit will break down."

Providing Support for Flawed Behaviour

"I will always provide support for the people who do their duty correctly. If they start to show flaws in what they're doing, it's better to provide support rather than cutting them loose in the early stages. I prefer to start by asking if the individual has been provided with the right training. It might be that additional training is required to get the individual up to speed. There's no problem with that at all, providing that I can see a desire to improve and people are striving for excellence with an understanding that I will not accept mediocrity! Supporting people to achieve excellence is what's important."

Must-Not-Haves

1. Do Not Use the I Word

"Most importantly, drop the I word! If you're talking about me, me, me, and I, I, I, and saying 'I have vision,' and, 'I want this,' and 'I want that,' people will switch off. It all becomes all about you.

"So it's got to be, 'What is my role in helping us achieve a collective vision?'

"It's okay to start with 'I believe that we can achieve,' because that's providing support for the general mission. But it can't be about, 'I want to be a head coach of the best team in the world.' You've got to take the ego out of this and make a collective statement that has people thinking that this is something we are going to achieve. I believe too much use of I will undermine leaders really quickly, as the perception will be it's all about them. Drop the I word!"

Use the I Word Only In a Support Role to Others

"It's okay to use it in a support role to someone else, to say, 'I will support you, because I believe what you're doing; therefore my behaviour will align with what you want to achieve; therefore I'm supporting you to do it – but this is a collective thing. I'm going to help you achieve our goals.'"

2. Do Not Tolerate Non-Compliance

"Once the program is set up and running, if you accept and tolerate non-compliance, you are stating publicly that you are going to accept compromise, and then you won't get success!

"If there is any compromise, whether it be through the training of your staff, the training of your athletes, the training of behaviour, acceptance of attitude, any of those things that are non-compliant with the team expectations and behaviours, it will compromise your outcome.

"When you get that cultural attitude against non-compliance, the athletes do it themselves."

You have to facilitate the development of your team:

"You've got to develop expectations and understand your roles and your responsibilities. Once you've identified the behaviours and responsibilities, and your expectations, then you must comply with them.

"As a leader, you really become your own compliance control manager. You identify people who are not being compliant early on and adjust their behaviours. This keeps everybody on track. It's not about leading from the front and saying, 'Follow me!' You've got to present the example, sometimes just walking behind or beside someone, and just giving them a tap on the shoulder to say, 'That's not what we expect.'

"When you instil a cultural attitude against non-compliance, the athletes maintain it themselves. As an example, our athletics team embraced the vision of what we could achieve at the Sydney Paralympics when 2.5 years out we became the number one team in the world and we discussed what was possible for the athletics Team in 2000."

A team dinner that they had before they left Birmingham was a good example of this in action:

"We had a team dinner before we left Birmingham to return home and I spoke about going to the Sydney Paralympics in front of our home crowd. I pointed out that being the number one team in the world after the 1998 World Championships in Birmingham would not matter if we couldn't replicate the result in Sydney.

"I'll never forget sitting at the table with a group of athletes, one of the athletes had had a couple of drinks. He was one of the ones who tended to have a few too many when he let loose. It was also the year I realised we had changed the whole culture of expected behaviour for elite performance.

"During the evening this athlete was drinking his beer and another athlete suggested that he wasn't serious about Sydney. He asked, 'What do you mean?' The response: 'Well that's your third beer! If you're going to start drinking two years out of the games, then you may as well forget being involved in this team.'

"I saw the athlete push the glass away and didn't finish it for the rest of the night. It was peer pressure to say you better step up your mark, because that's not good enough for our team any more. And that was fantastic!

"Without a word being said by anybody else, that moment stood out for everybody sitting at that table. That was the defining moment for stating what was expected culture within the team. That it was no longer the staff telling the athletes what's expected, they were exhibiting the behaviours that were compliant with excellence and that's what we absolutely loved about it; that exact moment defined the whole team."

3. Never Accept Mediocrity

Coming out of this, it is very important never to accept mediocrity:

"You do have to provide support to get the job done, and it's about understanding the background of where people come from. There is no place for people who work to rule. You can do that in a public service, you can do that in a school environment, you can do that in environments where if it doesn't get done today it's not life and death, because a lot of the things they have to do aren't defined by time.

"In sport, there is a defined time when things have to be done. Whether it is a world championship, Olympic Games or Paralympic

Games, you know that you have to deliver at a given moment. An athlete who is given a ball in the last moments of a game has to make a decision; an athlete who has to perform over a certain distance in athletics has to perform. The clock does not wait for them to be ready."

Success in team sports is about making decisions on the fly and being able to perform on demand:

"As coaches we don't want people who are mediocre in elite sporting environments asking, 'What should I do?' If that is occurring, it is a reflection of mediocrity in either the training of those people or the identification of them in the recruitment process. Elite sports staff must be confident in making quick decisions and complying with what is expected of them in their role. If you have people that I refer to as mediocre, they will ultimately compromise your environment.

"If I'm going to a team environment that has to produce an outstanding outcome and I have to call on somebody at two o'clock in the morning to take an athlete to hospital, or to sit with me for three hours and talk about how we've got to do something different, how we've got an athlete who's off track or who needs support, I need to be surrounded by staff who have the same drive for success as I do."

4. Do Not Leave Things to Chance

"You must not leave things to chance. If you do, it's accepting tolerance to non-compliance. It's letting people do things their own way, and it restricts the ability to predict the unexpected. A really good leader has the ability to bring the team together and sit down and say what is expected – how compliance is important to the team, and how it will assist with predicting what will happen.

"If this is done effectively – by a team leader with an excellent understanding of the sport – a plan can be implemented aiming at elite performance, including several options (depending on human and financial resources). If you're planning to prepare an athlete for a 100 metre race in athletics or swimming, there are very few things that you cannot predict. If you are planning for an athlete who is going to be skiing down a hill, in excess of 100 km an hour, with wind and snow conditions that are different at the top of the hill to the bottom of the hill, there are an infinite amount of things that can vary.

"You could catch an edge on the way down the slope and ski out of the course; you could come loose from your bindings and lose a ski; you could straddle a gate. There are so many things that can happen so you've got to be in a very, very different space to that of the controlled environment of athletics and swimming, in particular, which are generally the most closed environments you can operate in."

Bianca Chatfield – Australian Netball Team

Building Relationships, Integrity, and Empowerment

A professional netball player from Australia, Bianca Lee Chatfield was only 18 when she was selected for the Australian team to tour England and New Zealand. She has played for both the Melbourne Vixens and Melbourne Phoenix.

The Australian national team won silver at the 2006 Commonwealth Games and in 2007 they won gold in Auckland at the world championships. She is considered a world champion and is currently vice-captain of the Australian Diamonds and captain of the Melbourne Vixens; Bianca also led the Melbourne Vixens to victory at the 2014 ANZ National Championships.

Interview

Must-Haves

1. Building Relationships and Investing Time into Team Members

"My first experience in netball at the elite level was as a 16-year-old playing for Melbourne Phoenix – I was around some great leaders. I was 10 years younger than the majority of them but they cared about me as a player, and as a person, and it was an incredible club to be around – and a very successful club, as it turned out.

'When I was 18, my first experience in the Australian team was very different. The supportive environment I was used to wasn't a part of the Aussie team culture. The experienced players did what they needed to do, but wouldn't invest much time, if any, in the younger players. I didn't feel like I was a valued member of the team, just a young player coming along to train with the team.

"And yes I was young, and still very, very raw as a player, but it was the total opposite to what I felt with Melbourne Phoenix.

"That's what I base my leadership on now. Part of my leadership is to always make sure that you invest time and get to know all the people around the team. Not just players, but staff as well – you never know when you'll need them. You never know when you're going to have to put them onto the court. If you spend time getting to know everyone, figuring out what makes them tick, knowing what helps them on court, it becomes a far more enjoyable experience for everyone, and a much more successful team to be a part of."

2. Being True To Myself

Bianca Chatfield then spoke about what makes people tick, what their weaknesses are, and what they're anxious about:

"My second must-have is about being true to myself. So not trying to be somebody else, or not trying to act like other captains of the past.

"I think people can really tell when you're being authentic and genuine. That's when you earn the trust and respect from those around you. I've had experiences where I've been co-captaining teams, or when you're replacing someone as captain, and people expect you to act the same way. I don't think you can ever replace people. Identifying what your true values are, and then consistently living and breathing them, will get you more input from everyone around you."

She then spoke about being open with your mistakes:

"You shouldn't worry too much when you do make a mistake, because I think it allows people to see that you're real and you're human when you can admit to your mistakes. And that's on and off the court.

"I'm the first person who, when I play a bad game, will put my hand up and say, 'I'm sorry. It was my fault.' And then I need to show that I'm doing something about it. That's exactly what I would expect from the girls in my team, to first feel comfortable with self-reflection on their performance, and then show that they are doing everything they can to fix the problem."

3. Empowering Those Around Me

Chatfield was asked to describe her third most important must-have for team success:

"Just empower those around you! Don't be a leader that comes in and does everything for everyone. Allow every single person in the team to have some kind of bond to what the team needs to do. Whether that's when you're setting your values and behaviours at the start of the year; whether that's giving everyone some kind of a role or position description within the team. It's not just what they do on the court; everyone has to invest in the team off the court too.

"So we often do that. We split everyone in the team into mini roles. It could be as small as being the social coordinator; taking control of the warm up at training; or organising some of the off-court activities. This takes the pressure off the captain having to be the main voice all the time."

This is both at an international level and at domestic level:

"We're doing that at both national and international level. It works quite differently. With the Vixens, in Melbourne, I'd spend December through August working on this aspect of empowerment. Therefore it's a big chunk of the year that you get to spend with those girls. You come into the Australian scene by August and you're done by November. You're only there for three months and there isn't much time together as a team."

4. Live and Breath Success

"You've just got to love it!

"I strongly believe that leading by example is about having to live and breathe what you expect the team to live and breathe. And that's being a positive influence and always having some kind of optimism about how you are and how you think and how you talk. Because it does brush off onto the team around you.'

'We all know people who would drain us, negative people in our lives who zap all the energy out of you. I believe the leader of the team has to be the one who adds energy and vibe into the group and it will spread like a virus. When you're on tour with the Aussie team and away for weeks at a time you do get sick of travelling and living in hotels, it just becomes hard work. We have a thing that you've just got to love it! So if anyone's whinging, tired, or emotional, you've got the opportunity to turn around and say, 'Love it!'"

Must-Not-Haves

1. Don't Create a Hierarchy

"Don't create a structured hierarchy. I understand that you have to have a captain and a vice captain for organisational purposes. If they want to have a captain or a vice captain that's fine, but I don't like people being treated by where they stand in the hierarchy. And it goes back to my first experience as an Aussie player and how I felt I was treated.

"I didn't feel like I could speak up! I was a really shy kid and I didn't feel a part of that team. And so I think when you create hierarchies you allow people to act and to behave wherever they are on that hierarchy. So if they are the youngest member of that team and the most inexperienced you allow them to be pigeon-holed into that space, and that might mean they don't need to give back to the team and talk up at meetings, because it's their first year. And I think why have those barriers up for them? They can if they want to. I think you see now, in different generations, the younger girls are more confident, and are willing to speak up, and I love that – I try to embrace that."

In one experience, Chatfield relates how she went about getting rid of a hierarchy to solve a problem:

"Well, the way I tried to do it when I took over the captaincy of the Vixens a couple of years ago was that I introduced the position descriptions for each player, so that everybody had some kind of role in the team even when they were off the court. After that it wasn't just about what they did on the court, but it was about everything else as well, and making sure that in team meetings it was a collective of everyone having to contribute in some way. All of this was just a non-negotiable."

2. Don't Be a Negative Influence

Leaders often need to do a lot of things that they are uncomfortable with, and Chatfield has a good strategy for dealing with this:

"Surround yourself with positive and uplifting people. A leader definitely has a lot more pressure on them than most and you have to be able to deal with it.

"You have to take on an extra workload as a leader, and that's fair enough. You have to do it with a smile on your face; sometimes it's the last thing you want to be doing, but picking and choosing the right people to vent to is how you cope in these times.

"Don't be negative. Don't blame others. I think you have to put yourself out there and admit when you're wrong and create an environment where everyone becomes very self-aware. You always have to give feedback to yourself around your own performance. I'm talking on and off the court – before you ever think about anyone else. Whether that's taking time after a game to do that, or just encouraging that kind of process to happen, but some steps need to be taken so self-reflection becomes a priority."

3. Give Feedback So That It's Received Well

Feedback is an important part of the winning team process, but if it is too negative it can have the unintended effect of driving the team apart:

"You've got to do feedback in a way that you hopefully know that person well enough to understand how they like getting feedback. I know from my personality, I love honesty and I love directness and I don't want people to beat around the bush. But I can tell you there's probably four other girls in my team that need it put in a nice way – that's fluffed around a lot of positive stuff: … *but it's just that I'm going to give you this*; that you're doing this really well, and keep doing this, and try doing this for me. Frame it in a way so that they don't become defensive!"

You don't always have the information about a player's personality before you need to give feedback:

"In this situation it gets rather hard, but I think you always have to go back to the feedback and the solution to the problem rather than anything else.

"*This is what I'm thinking; this is what can help you* rather than *this is what you're doing wrong*. Once you've got to know the people, you can fine-tune the details. But if you don't have that opportunity, then feedback has to be as genuine as it can be. Be ready to provide the support as well as an explanation as to how they can do it better."

4. Put Your Team-Mates Before Yourself

"It's very important as a leader to put the team first. I think as a leader you have to make decisions at crucial times, but you have to have taken the time to hear other people's thoughts and opinions, Then work through making your own decision on what you think is right for the team, not you!

"To do this you can't just come into the group and all of a sudden go in a new direction because that's what you believe. You can't put your ideas first. You have to at least seek information and feedback from all the girls before you can stand up there and make a decision on their behalf."

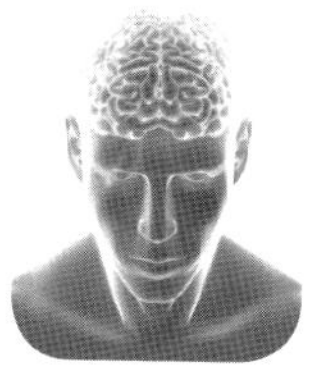

CHAPTER 5

A New Chapter in Sport and Business

It is the energy inside of the person that – when it is kept clean or clear – gives them the enthusiasm and passion to be able to display their skills. When the skies darken, that is the time they have to recognise that they have to step up, clear themselves and then go forward again. Because the ones that go down are the ones that are saying they are going to ignore the danger signs. *I'm just going to keep pushing myself.* When they do that what you get is injuries. Their mental systems lack enthusiasm, which equates to an increased level of complaining and back-stabbing. Drugs can become an alternative, both recreational and performance enhancing (and booze). There are signals. The signs are there for people who are competent enough to see it and pick up on it. We need our leaders in sport and business to change their mentality and listen to what is being said to them. One of the major problems in sport is due to the fact our athletes are being paid so much money, and lauded in the newspapers, and heralded wherever they go. Their ego has climbed so high that they can't be reached. So when they get dumped they have then got the painful climb back down.

In the world of elite golf Tiger Woods recently went through the drama we are currently talking about. This is a classic example of an athlete flying too high, then getting their wings singed from the sun. Very soon there is a collapse of a monumental proportion, and then they are out of the game (until such times as they decide they are going to start to rebuild their previous attitudes). The internal part of this golfer got so big he couldn't handle it – so he blew apart.

The golfer, with his wayward antics, was subconsciously craving to collapse so at some stage he could go back to living a decent life – one that did not offer the same levels of mental pressure – which prompted his downfall.

This fall from grace could have been avoided if he had been given strategies to clean up his mental garbage, which was increasingly mounting to the point it was overflowing and in need of an urgent clean out. For this athlete, and any other athlete, to maintain the levels of mental energy we talk about they have got to do the clearing of the septic tank. If you live in a house where you don't have sewerage, and you've got a silage tank that catches all the waste that goes through your kitchen sink, you have to clean it at least monthly. If you don't the next thing that happens is the sludge comes back up through the hole in the sink. And then that's all you've got: a sink (or mind) full of sludge.

So you've got to learn to clean out the areas that are debilitating the system.

Another example of this is a certain elite Australian female tennis player. When she is clear she can beat the best in the world, and the next day she goes out after beating the best in the world and she gets beaten by a so-called nobody. Why? Because her mental area is not clear, and her mental areas have never been clarified. So until such times as they are prepared to sit down with qualified people (whom are not sports psychologists) then they will continue to be brilliant one day and poor the next.

The sad thing is that those that are up in the elite world now can be past the point of recall. It's the young ones coming through that the clubs and institutions in Canberra need to seriously focus on with this new approach. In our opinion, it is these institutions and clubs that have to realise that if they want their students to be the best in the game – across the world – then they have got to put into place these new mentalities and methodologies.

In this day and age we should not have elite athletes breaking down, at any stage of the year, especially with the quality of physical human science now in place around the world.

The physical and mental components must be equal in strength to become a champion performer. If mainstream psychology worked in practice to the level that it should in theory then our jails should be decreasing in population. In reality they are dangerously bursting at the seams in all regions of this planet.

There is a new level of intelligence in this area now available. This increased level of performance and energy we talk about is exemplified by a greater level of intelligence. The intelligence we talk about is having a greater level of understanding of oneself. Of who we actually are; not what we and other people think we are. Because if we buy into what people think we are, our egos go out of sync with the rest of the brain system. In other words, you've got what they call an elephant in the room. And when there is an elephant in the room, there is not much room for anything else.

CORPORATE, GOVERNMENT AND SME SERVICES – ENGAGE & GROW

The organisational challenges that you are facing right now will suddenly soon be a thing of the past, and we are very excited about the possibility of demonstrating this to you.

Our break-through program is a specialised 'ALL-ACTION' system that will:

- Effortlessly improve engagement levels
- Strategically develop leaders on all levels
- Increase customer satisfaction
- Eliminate departmental silo mentality and create a dynamic flow of communication
- Create true accountability in all workplace deliverables
- Expand inter and intra team communication and collaboration
- Combat key day-to-day operational challenges.

We also proudly offer

- 100% Satisfaction Guarantee
- A comprehensive post program report, which will substantiate your return on investment

Our team of Certified Engage & Grow Business Coaches have over 100 years of expertise. We offer new, unique, and proven action oriented in-house programs which build individual and team engagement, accountability, motivation, leadership and performance in 12 to 16 weeks. For more information please email richard@engageandgrow.com.au or visit **www.engageandgrow.com.au**.

Twitter - richard_maloney

Linked in - richardmaloney1

Skype - richard.maloney8

Facebook - Engage & Grow

ENGAGE & GROW

ELITE SPORTS TEAM SERVICES – PREMIERSHIP COACH

After the initial planning stage, we go about fast-tracking your team's unity to effortlessly build more team players and re-educate the individuals. This creates fusion and accelerates organisational flow, bringing sudden and long-term success. Our programs range in time pending required outcomes.

We work with all or selected management lines, such as:

- Senior Executives
- Middle Management
- Staff Members
- Coaching Group
- Entire Playing Group
- Support Team.

Having now been involved in winning 24 'premierships' or 'championships' from 39 grand finals, we understand firsthand how powerful it is to have all levels of the organisation 'flowing' to achieve break-through levels of success. For more information please email richard@premiershipcoach.com.au or visit **www.premiershipcoach.com.au.**

Twitter - richard_maloney

Linked in - richardmaloney1

Skype - richard.maloney8

Facebook - Premiership Coach PL

INDIVIDUAL SERVICES – QUALITY MIND

For elite athletes and business leaders who want to become an inspirational leader for others through promoting new methods of thinking, which enhance greater benefits in the areas of health, wealth, and relationships.

The experience we speak of offers:

- A growth of consistency and integrity in self
- Direction and clarity with a clear vision to achieve your dreams
- Superior levels of energy and focus
- Mental strengths that easily overcome what are seemingly precious difficulties
- A building of self-worth, entailing a greater understanding of who you truly represent, where you are now, and what you are meant to become.

This exclusive program is designed to meet the needs of serious people looking to dramatically advance their present positional performances. Whether the emphatic increase required to kick-start new levels of energy is centred in business, sport, or general life arrangements, a freshly activated impulse of some greater element of cognition must be introduced and meshed into the present system. For more information please email richard@qualitymind.com.au or visit **www.qualitymind.com.au.**

Twitter - richard_maloney

Linked in - richardmaloney1

Skype - richard.maloney8